Rising Above

Business Leaders Going
Beyond Boundaries to Grab Success

Copyright © 2018 Vickie Gould International, LLC. All rights reserved.

This book or parts thereof may not be reproduced in any form, stored in any retrieval system, or transmitted in any form by any means—electronic, mechanical, photocopy, recording, or otherwise—without prior written permission of the authors or publisher, except as provided by United States of America copyright law.

This anthology project was led and compiled by Vickie Gould, Law of Attraction Business and Book Coach. www.vickiegould.com email vickie@vickiegould.com

Cover by: Michael Corvin
Edited by: Andrea McCurry

Co-authored by

Vickie Gould, Law of Attraction Marketing and Book Coach

Zinna Davis, Forgiveness/Faith Builder Coach

Brooks Gibbs, Author & Mentor

Dr. Joy Lough, Founder/ CEO of Joy Lough Enterprises, LLC, Journey Coach

Curtis G. Marsh, President/CEO Capital Growth Management

Janis Melillo, Transformation/Wellness Health Coach, International Best Selling Co-Author

Lisa Nielsen, Benefit Specialist and Educator

Dr. Emmanuel Nwoye, Business and Spiritual Relationship Coach, #1 International Bestselling Author

Jane Richardson, PhD Communication Consultant, Expert Witness, #1 International Best Selling Co-Author

Sherrod Schuler, Minister/ Speaker/ Corporate Change Agent

Sandra Stachowicz, Transformational and Empowerment Coach

Stacie Winkfield, Fairy Brand Mother and Social Media Strategist

Laverne Wyatt, Diversity Marketing and Branding Specialist

Do you dream of one day becoming a published author? Do you want to make your mark and have a lasting impact? Do you know that there are people out there waiting on your message?

Then, **I'd like to invite you to participate in the next anthology** and become a Best Seller like the authors in this anthology.

All you have to do is turn in your story and I'm going to give you easy-to-follow steps to writing it so that it speaks to those people who need your help. I'm also going to take away the tech overwhelm by publishing the book for you and guaranteeing the Best Seller status. Plus, I'm even going to have your story edited by my team.

Go here for details on the next project:
http://bit.ly/nextanthology

Acknowledgement

Thank you to all the authors in this book who were willing to share their journeys. It's always a humbling experience to compile and anthology with people like you. With your help, this book can create a positive impact on the world.

As always, extra special thanks to Andrea McCurry for dedication to this project and editing everyone's stories. This book could not have been put together without you.

Table of Contents

Acknowledgement 5
Dedication 8
Introduction 9
Trading Guilt for Power by Vickie Gould 12
Words of Wisdom from a Late Bloomer About Becoming an Entrepreneur by Jane Richardson 20
Lewis and Clark – Lessons on Entrepreneurship by Brooks Gibbs 30
One Word by Dr. Joy Lough 40
Confessions on Why Shift Happens by Janis Melilo ...46
Running Life with a Purpose! Be Exceptional! by Sherrod Schuler 56
Remember Who You Are by Stacie Winkfield 64
Design Your Life by Laverne Wyatt 72
Business and Relationships Built on the Rock by Emmanuel Nwoye 80
Wisdom of the Creek by Lisa Nielsen 92
Not Good Enough to Live, Too Good to Die by Sandra Stachowicz 100
Time Brings a Change by Zinna Ary-Davis 110
Creating and Rising Above the Chaos by Curtis G. Marsh 118

Dedication

Dedicated to all those who have a dream of entrepreneurship. We've fallen down too many times to count and it's our hope that through sharing our lessons with you, you'll be encouraged to pursue your passions through your lessons as well.

You truly can have the life that you want and we encourage you to go after it!

Introduction

The only difference between stumbling blocks and stepping stones is how you use them - anonymous

Everyone has a story - one with ups and downs and lessons to be learned along the way. No one is immune to failures, but it's the way that we view our failures that create success.

In "Rising Above," 13 entrepreneurs share their stories with you because we know our stories are not meant for us to keep to ourselves - they are meant to be shared with the world so that all can learn from our lessons as well.

When we fall down, it's our chance to learn and grow. If you've ever been around successful people, you see that they approach failure with excitement because they know that it's one more step towards their goals. It's not viewed as a bad thing and it's definitely not viewed as a reason to give up – it's a reason to keep going.

They get back up and go after their desires with commitment, optimism and focus, knowing that what they want is totally achievable.

The stories within this book are meant to share what we've learned in our businesses and I hope that you are inspired by them. Read them in whatever order you wish as the titles appeal to you.

Please know that the spiritual views of each author is their own and does not reflect the beliefs of the rest of the authors in this book.

I'd love to hear your feedback and how this book has impacted your life. Please leave us a positive review on Amazon and write me at vickie@vickiegould.com if you'd like.

Trading Guilt for Power

By Vickie Gould

"Yes, of course I can do that," and I smiled a huge smile, feeling that I was needed.

"Yes," was one of my most popular responses when someone asked me to do something.

I felt guilty if I said, "No," and yet all the "Yes" answers created stress and a need to constantly rearrange my schedule.

Most of my life I felt better making myself feel bad for the sake of others. Because I said, "Yes," so much to others, I was constantly saying, "No," to myself. Somewhere deep inside me, I wanted to speak my mind. I wanted to say what I really meant. I wanted to quit putting myself last.

It was as if every time I said, "Yes," I was also telling myself that I wasn't worth standing up for. That made me feel bad.

I gladly accepted the title of "Superwoman" and joyfully brushed people off with, "Oh, it's no big deal," when they asked how I was able to do it all so easily with such a busy schedule of work and kids.

I was a self-sacrificing martyr for other people, and it filled my pride.

But deep inside I was dying. I didn't know how much longer I would be able to last. I was always looking for the break in my schedule to catch a breather. I'd tell myself, "Just make it to {insert date}," and it would be fine.

Inevitably something else would come up and I would be asked to do another task like paint the church classroom murals, fill in for the secretary, serve in the nursery, go on the kids' field trips, or volunteer in the classroom to help with a party.

And that's how it went, round and round.

I brought those same actions and answers directly into the start of my business.

Any time someone asked for help, I said, "YES!" Again, I felt needed, wanted, and helpful. I got complimented on my willingness to help. I had emails waiting in my inbox all the time. I felt purposeful. I felt sought after. I felt good about what I was doing for the world.

Until I didn't.

Then it felt like I couldn't keep up. I couldn't do enough. I was ignoring the important things in my life, like my kids and my husband, for people who seemed to not give a rip who I was. Usually it was an acquaintance or a friend of a friend looking for help. They didn't ask about me. They didn't ask if I had time. They assumed I would be willing.

And most of all, I felt used.

It was like the world knew, "Go ask Vickie, she won't say, 'No.' She doesn't know how." I worked dozens of hours helping complete strangers.

Don't get me wrong, they thanked me, but I wasn't able to make a living because I helped them for free. The problem was that I'm a sucker for a sob story. I love to help those who are downtrodden or have had come across hard times. I've been there. I understand. I want to help. But I barely made a penny from it all.

Then the big day came where I had to make a decision. Would I allow someone to actually rob me from right under my nose?

She came into my group program, eager, excited, and asking for a customized payment plan because she was a mom and in school. Of course, I said, "Yes." I elongated her payments. I bent over backwards so that she could join my program with payment that went past the program end date, just so that it was more affordable for her.

Then the email came that she was not going to be able to make any more payments because of health issues (Note: the issues were something very common for women, and not life threatening – in fact, I suffered from both myself). She hoped I'd understand that her health came first.

The problem was that entire program had already been delivered to her. She had logged into the program just the day before as well, even though she said she was too sick and could barely get out of bed or think, which led me to believe her message was a premeditated attempt to get out of the rest of the payments, and to download all the trainings before finishing her payments.

She told me she was unable to finish the program.

I really felt sympathy for her. I also felt like she was running away from her own dreams, scared her business wouldn't work out, making excuses for not completing what she started.

And I knew she had downloaded all my training.

All my proprietary trainings were hers now.

I checked her Facebook page out of curiosity. She was out on the town, participating in business events, and it was interesting how it seemed she was actually out of bed, being quite active, unlike she had claimed. Had she not thought I would look?

I had to make a decision on how to respond. There was a contract after all.

Would I let her rob me of my content WITH my permission?

I felt guilty for sticking to my contract.

I felt guilty for not fully believing her sob story.

I felt guilty for wanting to stand my ground.

I couldn't believe myself - was I seriously considering letting her get away with it?

Or was it time for me to finally say, "No," and say what I really wanted to say?

So, I decided that I needed to stand my ground. God never said I needed to be a doormat in order to serve others. In fact, allowing her to take advantage of me would teach other people to treat me poorly. I had shown the world they could walk all over me with their smooth talk, assuming it was fine with me when, in fact, it wasn't.

The point wasn't about the money. It was about standing up for myself.

A nicely worded, sympathetically crafted email was sent. Of course, it wasn't seen as sympathetic because the answer was,

"No." She called me names. She threatened my reputation. And yes, her reprimanding response shook me and made my heart race.

Deep down though, I knew that telling this woman, "No," was the highest level of service I could give her. I'm sure her requests in the past had gotten her what she wanted, but had also taught her that she didn't need to commit, that contracts didn't matter, that she could always get out of things later if she had a good enough story ...

... and that she could rob people with their consent.

And I knew for me that my decision concerning my response was a big turning point in my business. I'm so thankful for this test because I became much more unapologetic for the other things in my business as well.

My lawyer told me that it wasn't really worth going after her. The payments didn't amount to enough for the hassle of the court costs, plus she was out of the country. In the end, she cancelled her payments through her credit card company and I decided to let it go rather than hold on to the tension and negative energy; however, she was made aware that if she did use my proprietary process, I would use the full extent of the law against her.

What came out of this experience was that I set new stipulations regarding other aspects of my business. I decided that I would no longer take calls at all hours of the day for the convenience of others. I set a schedule for when I would take my calls, and only one time a week, in the evenings, with a rare call on the weekends.

I created restrictions on making specialized payment plans for people.

Now when someone says, "That's expensive," I say, "Yup."

I decided that there was nothing wrong with my pricing and that there was also no reason for me to reduce my price or elongate a payment plan for a sad story. Yes, to get coached by me personally may be considered expensive for some. That's the investment level that's required.

When someone believes that your service is expensive, that is from their perspective. That's their mindset. That's their limiting belief. It is not a reflection on your pricing. Even if it's true for them, it does not mean it's true for you or the next potential prospect you meet.

After all, you can't go into a department store and ask them to reduce their price because you have a story. You can't go to the grocery story and chug a carton of milk, then ask to pay later when it's more convenient for you and your other bills. If you want something badly enough, you just go figure it out.

And the client you get in the end will be all that much more committed as well.

Vickie Gould is a certified Law of Attraction Marketing and Book Coach. She helps her clients go from blank page to Best Seller and beyond.

As a result of working with her, Vickie's clients are able to grow their following, help others struggling like they once did, attract ideal clients, increase their income, and make the worldwide impact that they desire.

What makes Vickie's coaching different is her love of marketing which she uses to coach her clients on how to leverage their Best Sellers with strategies to get consistent sales and clients from their books.

Vickie has 7 Best-Selling books, including this one, and she has been involved and mentioned in numerous of her clients Best-Selling books as well. Her greatest joy is in seeing their message come alive in WORDS. Visit her at www.vickiegould.com

She lives with her husband and three kids, along with her addiction to superhero shows on Netflix.

www.facebook.com/vickiegouldcoach

www.facebook.com/groups/betherealdeal

https://www.instagram.com/vickiegould/

https://twitter.com/vickie_gould

https://www.linkedin.com/in/vickiegould/

Words of Wisdom from a Late Bloomer About Becoming an Entrepreneur

By Jane Richardson, PhD

It was 1953, and bouquets of white orchids adorned the altar when Joan and Bob married. Joan worked in the Assessment Bureau of City Hall, and Bob served in the U.S. Army. Their life together was blessed with four children, including three sons and one daughter. Raising happy, healthy children and establishing successful careers were two of their top priorities.

Like many others at that time, they thought their career paths were set in stone. They envisioned jobs with a company for decades, enjoying a level of achievement, then retiring and living out their golden years in comfort. Sounds lovely, right? However, that is not how their story evolved.

Instead, Joan and Bob's story focuses on the courage to navigate their careers in a different way. Always focused on one of their top priorities, Joan stayed home to raise happy and healthy children, while Bob entered the entrepreneurial arena. Although the risk of building a business and hiring employees was outside his comfort zone, Bob didn't let the fear block his focus. Rather, he took a courageous leap of faith and established a Real Estate and Insurance business. Joan and Bob, also known as my parents, have always been my role models for a happy life and successful career.

Since I was born into an entrepreneurial family, my parents, teachers, and friends assumed I would follow the same career path. Fortunately for them, my three older brothers quickly followed in my father's footsteps. Unfortunately for me, I struggled with the idea of becoming an entrepreneur.

The idea of entrepreneurship means different things to different people. To me, it means overcoming self-doubt, conquering fear, handling risk, managing failure, and hoping for success. In no way was I ready for that level of uncertainty at the age of 20 years old.

Suggestions About Becoming an Entrepreneur

Spending years avoiding the entrepreneurial arena, my career took many interesting turns. These turns included: college communication instructor, congressional intern, legislative assistant, Capitol Hill professional, pharmaceutical sales representative, jewelry designer, and philanthropist. Throughout each turn, I noticed a familiar set of skills commonly found in each job. Remarkably, this set of skills was identical to the ones my parents instilled in me. From entry-level positions to entrepreneurs, success requires these seven skills:

1. Effective Communication - Express ideas clearly and confidently

2. Leadership - Motivate and empower others

3. Integrity - Adhere to high standards

4. Work Ethic - Willpower to deliver quality

5. Teamwork - Support and respect others

6. Flexibility - Adapt to changing circumstances

7. Time Management - Prioritize tasks and meet deadlines

Despite feeling well-equipped with my skills for success, I felt like a failure in my career.

I felt completely confident with my passion for effective communication. However, I was unfulfilled and frustrated at the thought of missing my true calling in entrepreneurship.

Not knowing how to move forward made me feel isolated and disconnected. You might recognize the feeling: lump in the throat, pit in the stomach, and self-sabotaging beliefs. After wasting years making endless excuses and feeling like a failure, a career change was desperately needed. I had to do this for myself, so I finally decided it was time.

It was time to stop self-sabotaging. It was time to stop the unproductive beliefs in my head. It was time to stop doubting and start believing that success would happen, even though I had zero proof and no reason to believe it. I spent months reading books, seeking advice, and investigating success stories on entrepreneurial skills. While all this information proved tremendously helpful, in the end, success for me would be defined as simply believing in myself.

The moment I started believing in myself, the view from my dreary living room turned into a bright office space full of endless potential. It prompted me to finally take action. I declared out loud, "Today will be amazing. Today I will become an entrepreneur!" And, just like that, Clearly Communicating, LLC was created. Honestly, it was that simple because it was designed around the skills I already had within me. My business is a representation of what I stand for, and I wish I had the courage to do it 20 years earlier.

Naturally, I was nervous knowing the level of uncertainty ahead, but I persevered. The next step was to identify what my business would include. I began brainstorming and working towards defining my mission and vision. I realized that my personal success required the combination of utilizing my moral compass and the lessons I learned as a child. With that combination, I recognized that success requires these seven strategies:

1. Understanding that personal achievement is not accomplished by putting others down

2. Establishing a habit of serving others

3. Aligning health, relationships, and career

4. Accepting things that cannot be changed

5. Embracing the necessity for continued education

6. Nurturing the need to sacrifice for the greater good

7. Knowing that money does not measure your meaning

Just when I thought I was progressing well, the painful realization that my deceased parents were unable to provide further guidance based on their experiences took over. I felt lost, isolated, and disconnected yet again. You might recognize the reoccurring feeling: lump in the throat, pit in the stomach, and self-sabotaging beliefs. Only this time, I turned to others for direction through difficult stages. I learned from these seven entrepreneurs, success requires a leap of faith:

"Success takes communication, collaboration, and sometimes, failure."

~ Jessica Alba, Actress & Businesswoman

"It's failure that gives you the proper perspective on success."

~ Ellen Degeneres, Comedian

"I never dreamed about success. I worked for it."

~ Estée Lauder, Businesswoman

"The most courageous act is still to think for yourself. Aloud."

~ Coco Chanel, Founder of Chanel

"Don't be intimidated by what you don't know. That can be your greatest strength and ensure that you do things differently from everyone else."

~ Sara Blakely, Spanx Founder

"Don't you dare underestimate the power of your own instinct."

~ Barbara Corcoran, Entrepreneur

"Don't you ever let a soul in the world tell you that you can't be exactly who you are."

~ Lady Gaga, Singer

Words of Wisdom from a Late Bloomer

I understand the courage it takes to enter the entrepreneurial arena. Some of my most valued childhood memories involve the privilege of watching my parents bravely define their future. I also understand that you are not born an entrepreneur; rather you choose to become an entrepreneur. Some may call me a late bloomer, but I eventually found my way. The choice to become an entrepreneur changed my life, and I am proud to celebrate it 15 years later. My communication consulting business has flourished beyond anything I could have imagined. The best part? Believing in myself.

You may be wondering, "Ok, so that worked for you, but how do I accomplish this for myself?" I get it. Based on my previous experience, I profoundly understand what that question represents. Designed with your success in mind, I combined decades of lessons learned from my parents as entrepreneurial role models, along with other entrepreneurs, and my own moral compass to create simple steps to follow.

Skills + Strategies + A Leap of Faith = Entrepreneurial Success

Begin by asking yourself three questions:

Step 1.

Question: How do I get started?

Answer: Success Requires Skills

Focus on your skills. Believe in yourself. Define your goals. Face fear. Commit. Learn more. Empower yourself. Speak up. Ask for help. Clearly communicate. Pay attention to detail. Think outside the box.

Step 2.

Question: What do I need?

Answer = Success Requires Strategies

Focus on your strategies. Pursue what you love with deathless devotion and laser focus. Conquer challenges and solve problems. Provide outstanding service to customers and community. Serve locally and globally. Reflect on accomplishments and celebrate milestones. Set higher goals and dream bigger. Embrace leadership and integrity. Work hard and recognize your power during the process.

Step 3.

Question: What can I expect?

Answer = Success Requires a Leap of Faith

The crucial step is taking a leap of faith. And if you don't have your own faith, you can borrow some from me. I have plenty to share. A leap of faith means taking action. For example, it may mean believing that success will happen even though there's zero proof or an intangible outcome. Taking a leap of faith means different things to different people and you may take your leap of faith in your own suitable way.

This very moment, right now, is an excellent time to take a leap of faith and act upon your entrepreneurial dream. Don't put it off any longer. Don't be a late bloomer. Instead, dive deep into your core, delete excuses, stop doubting, start believing, and realize your potential. Be a representative of what courage looks like and do something that you always wanted to do. Be brave enough to define success in your own terms.

Like that beautiful day in 1953, when bouquets of white orchids adorned the altar, as Joan and Bob married and innocently began bequeathing their entrepreneurial legacy to me, I aspire to do the same for you. I hope to encourage each of you reading this today to realize your potential. I hope to inspire you to believe that you do have an amazing entrepreneurial future. I hope to motivate you to take a leap of faith, enrich your life and the lives of others around the world, and leave an entrepreneurial legacy for the next generation and beyond.

Final thought

Don't ever be afraid to shine. Consider this your gold-plated invitation to be a courageous and successful entrepreneur. Know that I will be cheering you on. Here's to your bright future!

Jane Richardson, PhD specializes in communication. She distinguishes between effective and ineffective communication and makes the complex message clear. In 2003, Jane founded Clearly Communicating, LLC which provides specialized communication solutions for entrepreneurs, private companies, government agencies, and legal communities. With decades of experience working as a Fortune 500 communication consultant, expert witness, Capitol Hill professional, college teacher, author, and volunteer, Jane had the pleasure of collaborating with many successful organizations including: IBM, a U.S. Presidential Campaign, the U.S. House of Representatives, Bristol-Meyers Squibb, Ortho-McNeil Pharmaceuticals, St. Jude Children's Research Hospital, Arnold Palmer Spirit of Hope, and Industrial Sales and Manufacturing.

Educated in the US and Europe, Jane has a strong understanding of the communication process including public speaking, persuasion, message analysis and delivery, clarity and comprehension, and verbal and visual coordination.

Jane also co-authored the #1 International Best Seller: *Courageous World Catalysts* now available at http://amzn.to/2vK4DUm

You may contact Jane at **www.clearlycommunicating.com**

Lewis and Clark – Lessons on Entrepreneurship

By Brooks Gibbs

The sunlight shimmered as it reflected off the rolling motion of the ocean waves. Over three years of preparation, planning, execution, and sheer determination to push through each day had brought us to this moment...We had reached the goal, the Pacific Ocean! Great joy and excitement truly filled my soul, yet there was also a feeling of loss, as my soul asked, "What is next? This cannot be the end! Life is to be lived, to be in pursuit of, and progressing, moving forward. What is forward now, now that I have reached my destination?"

I imagine these were some of the thoughts that passed through Captain Meriwether Lewis' mind as he and the expedition team sighted the Pacific Ocean on November 20, 1805.

Life IS a journey, not the reaching of a destination. It is a journey of Entrepreneurship. I know that the definition of an entrepreneur is someone who takes on the risk of organizing and building a business. Yet, I believe that the experience of life is just that, taking on the risks of daily experience to grow and profit from the experience. I know that you, like me, take on the unique challenges of life, whether you build a business or not. You face new challenges and take risks each day to progress through your experience. The rewards that you receive are valuable to you in many ways; some are financial, some personal, some physical, emotional, spiritual, etc. Each is a profitable reward of great value to you and those in your sphere of influence.

I share the story of Lewis and Clark with you because the joy of life is in moving forward toward a purpose. The rewards are the accomplishments and progress that are made while moving in the direction of your purpose. Joy is more than achieving a goal, as there is always another goal to work toward. I have found the experience of Joy is in knowing you are consistently moving in the direction that you desire and that is in harmony with you, your purpose, your skills, talents, and beliefs. Know that you are becoming more of the fullness that lies deep within you. When you move the direction that is in harmony with your purpose, you are filled with joy and excitement in the journey. The challenges that come, while difficult, are taken on with purposeful effort and focus; and as such, bring a greater joy as these obstacles are met, assessed, attacked, and subdued. As you progress through your journey, you create your legacy that lives in the hearts and memories of all who were and will be connected to your adventure.

Moving a direction that is not in harmony with your purpose brings a life experience that is filled with frustration, depression, anger, resentment, and remorse. Accomplishments made while moving away from your purpose and true direction are fleeting and hollow celebrations.

My desire in sharing this story is to open you to *seeking first the purpose of your life, here in this journey we call mortality.* Choosing into the belief of a mortal existence means you decide to believe you are more than a mere mortal, and that there is a greater purpose than the daily life you trudge through. Life is a gift of experience to open your understanding and discovery of who you are, what you stand for, and what your values are, that you desire to hone, polish, and perfect through this experience.

I chose to share an example of Entrepreneurship and Purpose-Driven Life as it relates to the Corps of Discovery Expedition that Thomas Jefferson commissioned, better known as the Lewis and Clark Expedition from 1804 to 1806. There are great lessons to be observed and incorporated into your life's journey that come from a simplistic review of this well-known historical expedition.

#1 Know Your Purpose in Life and Business

The purpose of the Corps of Discovery Expedition was to explore and map the unknown territory that lay between the edges of the Eastern settled regions of the American continent and the Pacific Ocean that bordered the Western side of the continent.

Herein lies the first and greatest lesson of this expedition. When you **KNOW YOUR PUPOSE,** you **KNOW YOUR DIRECTION!** Lewis and Clark knew they would head West! They did not know the path to take; there was no map, they only knew the direction. As long as they moved West, they knew they moved in the direction that was in harmony with their purpose, and they progressed towards this purpose. To move any other direction was futile! This would take them further from their purpose and harmony with their success. West to the Pacific Ocean was the purpose which they could use as the fuel to move them forward, even in the difficult challenges that were certainly a part of the journey.

Do you know your Purpose and your Direction? Take the time to ask yourself: Why am I here? What is my purpose in this journey of life (or my business)? What is the treasure that I seek? Once you find the answers to these questions, you will have your compass and be clear on your direction. You can then assess each step to know if it is in harmony with your purpose and therefore moving you forward in your journey. Use this principal in your life and business, as it is the foundation that will allow you to build successfully and joyfully.

#2 Prepare for the Journey

Once Lewis and Clark knew their Purpose and Direction, they began preparations for the Expedition. Preparations included researching and discovering all they could about what they might encounter, in order to prepare themselves and the team for the challenges they would face. Lewis and Clark took one full year to study, plan, and prepare for this expedition. When they embarked on the trek they moved into the unknown with a confidence that they were prepared and had faith in themselves, their team, and their success. Because of their preparation, the challenges they would encounter on their journey were simply obstacles they had not yet experienced.

The second observed lesson from the Expedition is to Prepare and plan for the journey that lies ahead of you. Then, what you will experience is not completely unknown. You can discover much about what you will encounter. To question and seek knowledge is the choice and action that takes you from a space of hope, where you leave all accomplishments to the will and whim of others and the environment, to a place of faith in the actions you have taken to build your confidence. Preparation fortifies your commitment in being what is required to move through the challenges that will surely come. All challenges are first conquered in the mind, and the results are brought to fruition through your faith in action.

#3 Assemble Your Team and Build Trust

A total of 33 people assembled as the team to prepare for Lewis and Clark's Expedition. Twenty-nine participated in the training camp in 1803, at Camp Dubois, the winter staging area in St. Charles, Missouri. Men of many skills assembled and united in the common purpose of the expedition. As a team, this purpose-driven expedition would be accomplished.

The knowledge, skills, strength, and experience of the collective team insured success for this expedition. They spent time together to build a bond of trust that would be the glue that held the men together in times of trials.

Toussaint Charbonneau and his wife Sacagawea were brought on the team to communicate with the Native American tribes that were encountered along the way. Sacagawea fostered connections with the indigenous natives to be mentors for the team, so the team could learn from the mentors' experience and wisdom where to go and what to expect in the areas that lay ahead. The natives lived and knew the territory and were a source of valuable information and experience to the success of the team as they traveled.

Learn from this example to assemble your team and build trust in each other. Find those in and out of your circle who have purpose and direction that are common with your own. Enroll them, as they will enroll you, so you may assist each other along the journey.

When you move into new and unexplored situations, seek mentors to instruct and guide you. Bring with you confidants you know and trust to help interpret what is communicated and to assist you in knowing how to act on the information that is provided. Not all information is valuable in moving you in your desired direction. Use advisors to assist you in the evaluation and determination of what you should and shouldn't do. As you trust in your team, you will find success even through the setbacks that come.

In times of trial, those you trust and hold close are the ones, who along with you, conquer the challenge. Those you do not trust will be a burden and distraction to your success.

#4 Consistent Daily Action is the Fuel to Progress

The Lewis and Clark Corps of Discovery Expedition was a journey of over six years, however it became a lifelong legacy that flowed from Lewis and Clark past their own time in mortality until today, over 200 years later. Very few purpose-driven adventures are short term and realized in a few months or years. The reality is they are lifelong pursuits, with ebbs and flows of movement over their lifespan. Knowing that there is not an end to the journey, how can progress be made and measured? Advancement is measured in the actions taken on a daily basis. Find joy in the journey and reward in the actions taken each day. Everyday there was some action taken to support the purpose and direction of Lewis and Clark's expedition. Not every day was a day of physical movement. There were many times that the party camped at a site, making no physical movement towards the Pacific Ocean, yet they took action to care for themselves and prepare for the future movements they would make when the time and environment were ready.

Winter was not the time for physical movement. It was the time for rest, planning, and preparation for the spring and summer, when great progress could be made. Life and business have cycles; there are times for preparation, and times for decisive and massive action. Each cycle has value and is appropriate in its season. To accomplish great things, the simple daily actions add up, and in hindsight, create the massive results seen through the perspective of time.

In your journey take consistent daily action. It is easy to fall into despair and feel no movement is made, especially in the winter cycle of your entrepreneurial expedition. Progress is only made in consistent action taken to support your purpose and direction. Realize and acknowledge that each action taken is extremely valuable in moving you forward. In today's instant information and gratification world, it is easy to be distracted if it seems that progress is not made. Negative thoughts quickly take over the subconscious, declaring failure when each day does not produce the expectation of exponential success. Unmet expectations lead to inaction, which fuels negative thinking and encourages further inaction. This cycle of thought is the pathway to frustration and despair, which leads your expedition on the path to failure. Know and hold to the truth that there is no failure when any purposeful action is taken on a daily basis.

#5 The Experience of the Journey is the Reward

The Corps of Discovery Expedition officially began on May 14, 1804, as the party left Camp Dubois in Missouri, to cross the unmapped American continent to the Pacific Ocean. On

November 20, 1805, the expedition team finally encountered the Pacific Ocean on the West Coast of the continent. While the excitement and celebration were exhilarating, I am sure the moment was short-lived as a reward. The true reward for the team, who consistently executed the choices and actions that were required to get them to the Pacific Ocean, was the knowledge and wisdom of the journey's adventure. The memories of the daily experience, the triumph over each challenge, and the connection to each other were the reward that each held onto in their heart and mind. The joy in the memories of what they accomplished along the way held the most value.

Our lesson here is that the true reward is the experience and wisdom that you gain in knowing your strengths and weaknesses and building the relationship with others. Do not be distracted by the belief that the destination is the reward and the ultimate value in your expedition of entrepreneurship. Wealth and riches can be acquired and lost however, the experience and knowledge of what you gained will remain with you eternally.

Joy is a feeling that comes from the perspective you place on your thoughts. Joy in the success for the expedition was created in the mind of Meriwether Clark long before the adventure unfolded as shown in his following statement.

> *Entertaining as I do the most confident hope of succeeding in a voyage which had formed a darling project of mine for the last ten years, I could but esteem this moment of my departure as among the most happy of my life.* — Meriwether Lewis

These are five simple lessons Lewis and Clark taught me in my experiences as an entrepreneur. I have ventured the path of entrepreneurship several times in my life so far. Some measured with financial success, while others crashed and burned when measured by the financial returns they generated. What I can say is that each path has been a great gift of experience for me to discover who I am and what I am here to be, learn, and reveal about myself. As a personal coach, I know that Joy is a much different feeling than happiness. Joy is long-term and soul felt; it remains with me even in my moments of challenge and despair. These moments of challenge are fleeting and are overcome when I reflect upon my journey and the success I made in following my purpose and direction. When my efforts in business and life are in harmony with my purpose, I truly experience joy.

As a Life Coach my purpose is to assist you in the discovery of your Joy by helping you to find your purpose and direction. Once you find this, you have the fuel to accomplish all you desire that is in harmony with your discovery. There are many mentors to can help you with the mechanics of how to create and build your business in your target market, however, the joy of your success will be realized when you discover your why, and your actions in life move you towards Your Purposeful Direction!

Brooks Gibbs is an international presenter, motivational speaker, personal and business mentor, and international author. More importantly he is a Lover of Life, Learning, and People.

Brooks sees the world we live in as our teacher. Simple examples in nature and life-experience teach great lessons that, when taken in, bring Harmony, Peace, and Joy to your experience. These lessons open your heart to know that there is always a path to follow; there is always an answer to be received; and there is always a friend and mentor to love and support you through the many transitions and challenges of life. He brings these Little Lessons of Life to you in simple and effective stories that teach principals of how to make the journey of life an experience of joy.

Brooks believes in "digging in" and working with you to turn challenges into triumphs. Through his "Gentle Soul and Healing Heart," he helps individuals to open their minds and thought processes, by asking the right questions and encouraging them to find their own unique answers to the challenges they face.

Brooks will help you realize that the road blocks and walls of life are first solved by opening up your thoughts to new possibilities and stepping into trust. He will help you realize that you can move through the challenges with a new direction that comes from within yourself. Contact Brooks and begin the journey of positive change in your path.

Email Brooks at: www.brooks.gibbs@littlelessonsoflife.com

One Word

By Dr. Joy Lough

She is a mocha, caramel-skinned woman with natural hair and an infectious smile. She has a personality that exudes confidence, love, and care. She is an author, a motivational speaker, and a business consultant. She is determined. She is courageous. She is victorious. She is beautiful. She is me.

Just a few years ago, I was so different. Back then, I was someone who cried constantly because of "life."

Press Rewind...

I was desperately trying to complete my dissertation on successful entrepreneurship, because it was this dissertation that would make me the "expert" in my field and move me and my business to the next level. Or would it?

The dictionary defines *expert* as a person who has a comprehensive and authoritative knowledge of or skill in a particular area. Could a document with 100-plus pages equate to that? An expert? Me? With an authoritative knowledge?

These thoughts of doubt and uncertainty became permanent residents in my mind, and I couldn't seem to evict them no matter how hard I tried. It took me seven years to complete my dissertation, and so many times along the way, I asked myself, is it worth it? Should I continue? There were so many obstacles including late nights doing research, getting laid off from a job that I absolutely loved, then trying to find work to provide for my children, and being a single mother. There was no support from family or friends as they provided constant, giant reminders and whispers of, "You always think that you are better than us," and "You are doing too much." **I wanted to quit.**

The thought crossed my mind -- maybe I should write a dissertation on "life," because I could use the expertise on the topic. I could use the research where others survived what I had been through, what I was going through. I could use that authoritative knowledge, that motivation, that "You can do it" reminder.

Growing up, that positive role model or even mentor - I didn't have one. So, I was left to rely on total strangers to guide me through this milestone, this process of completing something so unfamiliar. Writing and researching my dissertation alone became extremely frustrating and exhausting, and let's be honest, it was HARD. **I wanted to quit.**

When my daughter came of age and questioned me about her father, I felt numb. Why did the teacher even have to assign a project where students had to complete a family tree? Did she not know or realize that there were so many single-parent households? Some doors should remain closed. We are in the 21st century. Where had she been? And how could she not take into consideration the possibility of a parent that might be deceased? I thought, "How insensitive is this assignment?"

I soon realized that my anger was not at the teacher, but rather aimed in a direction that I wanted so desperately to forget. How could I look at my daughter's beautiful face with those big brown eyes and her personality, so full of life, and explain to her that she was a product of rape? That she is still here because that's how much I love her? That I can't provide her the answers to question of who belongs on the left side of the tree, because I just don't know. Just the thought of that conversation. **I wanted to quit.**

And then there was my son who was prescribed some medicine that changed his mentality and changed my world -- again. He told me he didn't want to be here anymore. He said he felt like he needed out. And then he took an entire bottle of prescription pills. The doctors said, "Oh, that's just one of the side effects," as if he had a cold or cough. Suicidal thoughts! A side-effect. Imagine that. How could I comfort my son when I too was at a very low point? I felt ashamed – unjustly. I felt this sense of self-loathing. How could I go on? It was hard to get a grasp of what happening. There were so many nights that I could not sleep trying to figure out the "why" of it all. **I wanted to quit.**

A few years ago, I had a nonprofit working with underprivileged youth, teaching them music instruction. I felt so much joy when the children smiled and jumped at their accomplishments of finishing a lesson or learning a song. But when someone broke into the facility, they stole all the instruments and computers along with *everything else,* including a piece of me. **I wanted to quit.**

How could someone take from a child? It made absolutely no sense to me. And the board members, who were highly-recommended people and well-to-do in the community, just decided that starting over was too much for them. I felt sick to my stomach, like I had lost a child. This loss took a toll on me mentally, physically, and emotionally. **I wanted to quit.**

Fast forward...

One day while listening to an inspirational station on the radio, my life began to make sense. I realized that all the events from my past were all chapters of my "life" book. I had total control. I could easily turn the page and rewrite or edit pages at any time. But I had to choose to do so. I had to know and take ownership of my life, my book, my story.

It was then I decided that **quitting was no longer an option**.

I decided to write a book of poetry, and share my life's story. In the book, I talked about growing up, my children and family, my "why." There were specifically a few poems that talked about domestic violence. Because of that book, I was asked to speak on domestic violence awareness, first to churches, then to various organizations, and then to schools and other community events. I started working with local domestic-violence shelters and helping ladies with résumés, job preparations, and establishing an exit plan for their situations.

Sharing my story was therapy for me. At one event, I told my story, and a young lady called me a few weeks later to tell me that that she and her children safely escaped their situation because of MY story and advice. She said that I motivated her. I was so humbled.

There was another event where I spoke to a group of ladies on "Finding Your Why." I talked about my children and my life up until that point. A woman called me later that day and asked to meet me. She shared her story with me and asked that I mentor her in her business and life. A total stranger. She even agreed to pay me to do it. What a blessing!

In my books, I write about various topics such as being a single mother, starting over in relationships, business "blues," finding the right people in your life and in your business, etc. I know what not to do as an entrepreneur. I know who to trust, who to have on your team and who you need to leave in the background because they are just casting a shadow on your light. I know this NOW because of my experiences, and I choose to gift others with this knowledge. People buy my books and then ask me to speak. I facilitate workshops and seminars on business startups, development, and Human Resources. I have received contracts and a steady client base. I am so grateful! So many doors have been opened from just a few lines in a poem from my first book.

I see now that I HAD TO become that role model that I needed when I was growing up. I HAD TO find the strength, perseverance and fortitude to keep going when I wanted to quit so many times. I HAD TO be that person with the, "how I met myself," moment. I HAD TO complete my dissertation and be that EXPERT in business. I HAD TO learn to love myself even when others did not love me. I HAD TO do all of this, not just for myself, but for my children too. I HAD TO do this for the person reading this now.

A knowledgeable, professional, unwavering woman evolved from feelings of defeat and shame. Life presented lessons and challenges that demanded that I turn them into opportunities. I found my purpose when I accepted who I was. Who I am is a SURVIVOR of my past. And I realized that telling my story is what I must do…one word at a time.

Joy Lough, PhD is a motivational speaker, visionary entrepreneur, author, and business educator. With over 20 years of experience in entrepreneurship, business, and human resources, she is the CEO of Joy Lough Enterprises, LLC.

Their mission is to IMPACT lives professionally and personally through education, motivation, and inspiration. Dr. Joy assists entrepreneurs with the startup and development of their organizations and provides personal development for individuals. Dr. Joy is passionate about helping build and foster productive and prosperous members of society.

Dr. Joy has spoken and lectured at schools, colleges, universities, churches, and community events in a variety of venues.

For booking or more information contact:

info@joylough.com

336.223.4778

www.joylough.com

www.fb.com/joylough

www.instagram.com/joylough

https://www.linkedin.com/in/joylough/

Confessions on Why Shift Happens

By Janis Melillo

If you are ever in a position to change your life while helping others do the same, do it!

Mindset Shift Happens

Life is truly magical, filled with blessings each day. We breathe, live, and learn every day. Life is indeed so incredibly wonderful, yet at times difficult, tragic, and sad. We must remember that as each day passes, we have an amazing opportunity to change the world by being in one another's presence and sharing ourselves through our life's work and our passion to serve others. To be inspired is to share our triumphs and tragedies in ways we never thought possible. Say it isn't so, and I will show you a way to change your mindset and effectuate change all around you!

How in the midst of everyday life did change happen for me? Well honesty, I am still working on that change each day by starting out with my positive affirmations, journaling, and my daily dose of movement, a.k.a. exercise. My mindset in short, has been through a series of mistakes, misfortunes, blessings, and opportunities that I never saw in my pathway. A positive mindset shift requires staying the course and not veering off the path when things get tough.

I practice what I preach, stay the course, and veer off the path only when something does not feel right. I have been known to occasionally take the wrong road and when this happens I take a moment to reflect on all that is good and in abundance. I wake up each day and give 100%, even on the days when I feel I don't have anything more to give or something new or different to say. In other words, I dust off the cobwebs from the day before, and rise up, starting each and every day by giving it my all! I say this quite often but I finally figured out what I want to be when I grow up, and I am not going to take the easy way out like I formerly did throughout my life. An important lesson is that when the going gets tough, do not permit that toughness or ego to steer you down the route of self-despair and doubt. There may be a fork in that road down to the path of parts or places unknown. This is why taking the easy way out is not an option!

The easy way out for me always happened when I got to the point when it became evidently clear that I had to take a chance or have faith in my decision in whatever I wanted or whatever I was passionately working on. Instead of taking that chance, I ran in the opposite direction and just gave up. My mindset was not where it should have been.

When making any choice or decision to start a business, our frame of mind will not take us where our work ethic does not want to go. In other words, our actions must be aligned with our work and mindset ethics. You must be able and willing to put a whole lot of work into your business; very early mornings, late nights, and weekends, whatever it takes. You also need to allow yourself some down time, so schedule that in your calendar if you must, so that it coincides with your schedule. Writing your down time in your calendar is a way to ease your mind shift so that you do not feel like you are missing out on something or that you have too much to do. It allows you to be mindful and respectful of your own time.

When I started to build my business, I was excited and eager to move mountains (I still am!). What I lacked was the mindset shift I needed to be focused and detail oriented to complete the tasks that would catapult my business to where I wanted it to be. I kept myself busy and I did accomplish a great deal however, my shy-by-nature personality inhibited me from putting myself in front of an industry that I truly love.

I am a wellness/transformation health coach, and at the start of my entrepreneurial journey I felt I had to do and be everything for everyone. Well guess what? I took on way too much. Although my heartfelt intentions were certainly well placed, I just couldn't get out of my own way. Which program should I use? How do I install them? (I guess I am somewhat IT challenged.)

There had to be a better way for me to market myself and be more proactive versus reactive. Think about that statement for a moment and apply that to something happening in your life right now. Being proactive means doing the things that you know will hold you accountable to your goals, while being reactive is defined by the lack of time or knowledge on how to complete a task.

Being proactive came to fruition for me when I was faced with some recent medical issues that set me back for about 10 months. I had hip surgery and was laid up for quite some time. I had an abundance of time to think, strategize, and re-energize what I truly wanted for my business. What I desired more than anything for my business was to assist others on their path of wellness, but to do this I had to be willing to stretch my personality from shy to courageous, or as I sometimes say, I had to get out of my own way and get over my fear of being visible.

It is and always has been my love, loyalty, and determination to make a difference in someone else's life. I was meant to share my story through my own struggles and hardships, to be of service in the field I am so passionate about: wellness through fitness and nutrition. During my recovery I realized I had more to offer as a health coach by sharing another medical issue I was going through. Previously, I had been diagnosed with non-celiac gluten sensitivity. I learned that through my own adversities and health issues that I could make a difference to someone else going through the same type of health problems. That's how "The Gluten-Free Diva" was born. Diva to me stands for Divine Inner Vitality Always.

So, what is gluten? In very simple terms, gluten is a protein found in wheat, rye, and barley. Gluten is considered the glue that binds these types of foods together. For instance, gluten is found in bread, baked goods, cereals, and so many other food sources that you would never really know until you have a gluten issue. (See www.celiac.org for a more descriptive narrative.) Many other products have gluten in them as well, including medicines and healthcare products such as shampoos and lotions. Gluten is also found in some places I would have never imagined, such as lip balms, ice cream, deli meat and cheese, condiments, soy sauce, cosmetics, soups, ketchup, salad dressing, sauce, candy, and beer and liquor. (Visit www.glutenfreelabels.com - an amazing website with a lot of great information.

At first, I didn't know what was going on with my body. Why was I getting so sick an hour or so after I ate? It seems as though every time you nurture your body with what you believe is good food for you to eat, you may actually be poisoning yourself with food products that literally make you sick. Some basic symptoms of gluten sensitivity include nausea, bloating, abdominal pain, exhaustion, and chronic fatigue. This is just a small glimpse at the many symptoms especially women experience.

Having non-celiac gluten sensitivity led to major gallbladder issues for me. My gallbladder cannot process solid foods which contain gluten. As soon as gluten hits my gallbladder, it is just like sludge going through a car engine. I had severe gallbladder attacks. The pain was incredibly intense. My doctor wanted me to go to a surgeon to have my gallbladder removed. But, the right choice for me was to control my gluten sensitivity through my nutrition. I am thankful that I have the knowledge and skills as a certified health coach to assist anyone who is dealing with celiac disease or people just like me who have gluten sensitivity.

This moment was the beginning process for me on how mindset shift happens! I was determined that my sensitivity to gluten would be the catalyst of my shift to help and serve others with the same type of food sensitivity.

> *A shift in mindset has the ability to chase that which we are passionate about. It is a feeling so strong that you can visually see what the outcome is.*

There is no right time to start a new endeavor or business. Even when you already have a business up and running and decide to shift it in a different direction, or when adversity strikes and you are inspired by life events, that is when creativity lets you know to kick it up a notch. There are so many numerous decisions to make, the list seems never-ending. Visibility, branding, a new website, social media, which social media outlets are the best for your niche - just so many endless decisions to make.

In the midst of shifting my business and all of the little health issues that have popped up, I have had the opportunity to co-author 10 books. Mindset shift also happens in some ways that we never imagine and that in itself is such a blessing! Writing books is a new dimension and platform to share my expertise in the field of health coaching and gluten sensitivity. I am also in the midst of drafting my first solo book!

You don't write because you want to say something, you write because you have something to say. F Scott Fitzgerald

I believe I am now at a point in my entrepreneurship where I have something to say that will make a difference in someone's life through my work as a gluten-free health coach and as an advocate of wellness in general. The word "wellness" all by itself is a boring word, but wellness in the context of, "Healthy is the new Wealthy," is what really lights me up! Each and every one of us has the power to enhance or change the course of our health. We are genetically predisposed to some health issues, despite how well we take care of ourselves. Yet, I had the ability to say no to gallbladder surgery and control my gluten sensitivity through my diet. That is the sum and beauty of the idea behind, "Healthy is the new Wealthy."

I want to stress, do not go on a gluten-free diet because you believe it may be the next fad to lose weight and that going gluten-free is the ticket to achieve that outcome. For the many sufferers that have celiac disease or a gluten sensitivity, it is a long and lengthy overhaul process before being diagnosed. I endured all sorts of doctor's visits and tests galore. Since I have been diagnosed with a non-celiac gluten sensitivity, I feel a sense of accomplishment. I trusted myself enough to listen to my intuition which literally changed my health in such a way that I am able to motivate and assist others with the same gluten sensitivity issues to live and achieve a healthier lifestyle.

The beauty and power of what I went through while building my business, while still tackling my health issues, is that I had the power to change the outcome of my health, which shifted my perspective on my business and wellness. That shift in turn made me a much better advocate for my entrepreneurship. Shift happens in ways we never anticipate and again leads us on that path of self-discovery to reach out to others. Being a health coach has been the best decision that I could have imagined. Now I have a much more centralized focus on where and how I want my business to go!

Where do I want my business to go? Honestly, to infinity and beyond! This is again where your mindset must conquer and visit parts unknown. What the heck does that mean? It means your focus and determination must always have a way to assist others. When you have your health you have everything because without it what do you have?

For me this mindset means spreading my message that there's light in the face of adversity and wholesome nutrition to consume after you've been diagnosed with celiac disease or non-celiac gluten sensitivity. There are numerous ways to enjoy the transition into a healthier lifestyle while not feeling that you are deprived or that you may be missing out on something good to eat. There is a certain quality of life after gluten. I promise you that!

Wellness obtained through fitness and nutrition never sounded so good! Through adversity, we learn beyond what we think may be possible; we are challenged by that which we are meant to achieve in ways we never anticipated. Mindset shift happens when we are constantly put to the test. A shift can happen. I am living proof of that, and that is the beauty of life

Note to self: all you have to do is show up. Be late. Be scared. Be a mess. Be weird. Be confused. Just be there. You'll figure out the rest as you go. ~ Nanea Hoffman

 Janis Melillo lives in North Haven, Connecticut with her husband, Gary. She is a Transformation/Wellness Coach who works with women on their transformation path towards wellness through fitness and nutrition by implementing small changes leading to a healthier lifestyle overall. She is a certified health coach, having received her training through the Institute for Integrative Nutrition. She is a former licensed massage therapist and certified personal trainer.

Janis hosts a daily blog (Monday - Friday) on Facebook called FitnessDiva-411 where she shares her love of fitness and nutrition. She is also the host of three other Facebook groups: Circle of Hope, FitnessByDesign-411, and GlutenFreeByDesign-411, and is the owner of her health coaching business WellnessByDesign. Her Facebook business account is: @WellnessByDesign411.

Janis is also an ordained minister and recently started Digital Life Ministries, an on-line ministry which may also be found on Facebook. This is a non-denominational ministry that shares quotes and spiritual inspiration.

Along with fitness and nutrition, Janis loves to write, and two books she co-authored hit the International Best Seller List! Her third book was recently published, and she has also written articles for two different on-line publications.

Janis' website: www.WellnessByDesign.liveeditaurora.com
email: Janis@janismelillo.com.
You may also follow her on Twitter: @MelilloJanis.

Running Life with a Purpose! Be Exceptional!

By Sherrod C. Schuler

Do you not know that in a race all the runners run, but only one gets the prize? Run in such a way as to get the prize. 1 Corinthians 9:24 NIV

The very first time someone told me they had aspirations to run a marathon or any other long-distance race, I thought to myself, "Who does that?" and "Why?" At the same time, I had no idea an actual marathon consisted of 26.2 miles. I knew it was a lot of miles, but I did not realize it was run all at one time, by one runner. Although I was very impressed with any human being that could actually complete this undertaking, I was convinced this type of running adventure had nothing to do with me. This race was reserved for very exceptional individuals who had nothing else to do. In fact, statistically speaking, less than 1% of the U.S. population has ever run a marathon. I was not privy to know anyone in my circle who had completed this task.

You see I grew up in Flint, Michigan, where a great majority of my youth was consumed with basketball. In fact, a great majority of the young males I hung around loved the sport as well. Honestly, I thought basketball and football were the only sports reserved for exceptional athletes. And if I was told to run without a ball being involved, it was because I failed to follow instructions during practice. You see, running long distances for me was a form of punishment. I really didn't see the value or the purpose in it at all.

Nevertheless, as I looked for ways to improve my performance as a high school athlete, I stumbled upon running as a method of conditioning during the off-season. Running became a means to improve endurance and stamina for my "wannabe" basketball career in high school. In fact, I attribute running during this time as the "edge" I needed to land a roster spot when my skills and talent alone would not have gotten me anywhere close to making the squad. It was then that I realized running could have some benefits, but I still wasn't convinced it was a purely enjoyable thing to do.

Later, as my athletic career vanished and my life moved on, so did running. The purpose of running during my young adult years was non-existent. Therefore, I decided to hang up the old running shoes. I thought to myself that, I hadn't done anything wrong to put myself under this type of unnecessary pressure or punishment. Needless to say, I wasn't trying to make any roster spots. I just did not need to run, or at least that is what I believed.

It was during the winter of 2005, when life began to deliver a series of blows. The first blow came as I received a pink slip at a moment when I thought I was doing a fantastic job. However, my employer at the time seemed to think differently. They described to me the day I was fired, "The Company is currently restructuring. Effective immediately, your position is being eliminated." Of course, I didn't see that coming. I thought to myself, "I am doing what everyone else is doing. How is this happening to me?" I was correct; I was doing what everyone else was doing. You see I was doing average work and was not performing at an elite level. What I learned from this experience is that a few of my peers that did perform at top levels were actually promoted, while the mediocre performers were let go. It was the co-workers who were willing to go beyond what was expected that remained. Lesson learned.

The second blow came in late 2006, when I was served divorce papers while I was assisting a client on my new job. Talk about an embarrassing and awkward moment. Later, I would come home to a house that was cleaned out with nothing left, other than a daybed and my "money-green" couch. Suddenly, my newly constructed dream home became a divorced bachelor's crib. Oh, and did I mention my daughter was less than a year old at the time? This fact made the event most painful. Again, I thought to myself, "I'm doing what all the other young husbands I know are doing. How is this happening to me?" You see, I was being reactive to life's circumstances instead of being proactive in creating the world I desired for my life.

Then, the third blow came in 2007, when eventually I was no longer able to maintain the mortgage on my home. In fact, I was working two jobs and was still coming up short on this obligation. After agreeing to put the house on the market for sale, it eventually went into foreclosure due to being deeply underwater. Talk about a "financial crisis!" I began to let these events define my life. I was losing complete control.

I decided to move from Detroit, back to my hometown of Flint, Michigan. While trying to recover and rebuild, I felt stagnant. I soon realized I was just going through the motions.

I began searching for something that would renew my strength and change the circumstances I found myself in. I decided to lend my full attention towards my faith in Christ. This focus started a commitment toward a daily morning routine of prayer. As I began praying each morning consistently, I begin to feel in my spirit that I needed to be active and moving. Metaphorically speaking, it was as if God was telling me that I could not sit still, wallowing in my problems. Instead, I had to move forward. I had to begin to take control and own my own life. You see I had adopted the mentality that everything was happening to me and I had no control of the situation. But, I was responsible for what was happening, and I was the only one who could change it.

So in my restlessness to figure things out, I started running. At first it started out as a stress reliever. Slowly, I began to incorporate a short run as a part of my meditation time with God. Running became symbolic to me in the sense of moving forward with my life. Quickly, I began to notice how I felt more alert, more energized, and less stressed after each run.

In the beginning of 2008, with my lifestyle of running and prayer, things began to turn around. One of the first things that happened was an encounter I had with a Caucasian lady standing in the teller line at the bank, wearing running apparel. Intrigued, I inquired about her attire and was informed she had just completed a daily run. At that moment this runner fascinated me. Although, I was a novice at running, I was curious to hear from someone with experience. She seemed to enjoy what she was doing and was so happy to share her passion. She then invited me to join her running group. At first, I was hesitant, but I gave it some thought and decided, what the heck? I took her up on her offer and tried the group.

The group met once a week in various neighborhoods throughout the Flint area. The purpose of the group was to train for the annual 10-Mile Crime race. I had heard of the race a few times before, but never thought it was anything I would do. However, after joining the running group, I decided to participate in the race.

The group provided a support system and gave me insight and tips on how to be better at running. I learned what shoes to wear and what food to eat. I learned techniques on how to pace myself during a long-distance run as well as gained confidence in the fact that I could actually complete a ten-miler. Most importantly I learned the power of a mastermind group where I could draw from the strength of other like-minded individuals to help me not only reach my running goal, but to push me to go beyond my limited expectations.

Then one day, while perusing my company's intranet site, I came across a short trivia quiz about the history of the marathon. The page explained that one lucky winner who completed the quiz would be selected to win a free entry into the Chicago Marathon. Did I mention the accommodations included a Chicago downtown high-rise luxury hotel? I decided to take the quiz for the fun of it. And what do you know, I won the prize! I was so excited about being the winner. This was the first time I had ever won a drawing. I was ecstatic until I realized I won a prize to run a marathon! Huh? I guess I was lost in the moment. As I toiled over accepting the reward, I thought to myself, "This is an opportunity to stay in a beautiful hotel in Chicago."

So, on October 12, 2008, just before my thirtieth birthday, I embarked on a mission to complete my first marathon. Prior to this day, I had put in hours of training including a series of smaller races leading up to the big race. The main thing that I learned while training was to put one foot before the other and keep moving. I stayed focused by using the three P's: **prayer, prepare,** and **pursue**!

However on the day of the race, not knowing what to expect, I had a range of emotions. I wasn't sure if I was capable of this task despite all my preparation. I became overwhelmed. Although, I was physically prepared to run the marathon I began having negative thoughts. In fact, before the race I decided that I would run about 10 to 13 miles, then potentially veer off course to catch a taxicab somewhere in Chicago. I figured that Chicago was known for its plethora of taxicabs waiting to take people to their destination (at this time there was no such thing as Uber.) You see, I was self-destructing. I was talking myself into defeat before the race had even begun.

It was at this point, that I realized, the only thing that was stopping me from reaching my goal was ME. I began to change not only my mindset but also, my self-talk. I had **prayed** about this very moment, I knew I was well-**prepared**. Now it was time to show up! It was time for me to **pursue** the quest which I had been sent to complete.

I use this race and my experience with running to show you how you can apply this concept of the three P's to all areas of your life. Before pursuing any goal, I truly believe that it is important to start with prayer. Prayer provides clarity and insight into your purpose. It is in the purpose that you find and define your "why" and the "end-game." With my marathon experience, my end-game was to complete a 26.2-mile run in "Chi-Town." Before beginning that race, I had to be certain and clear of the destination and the goal I expected to accomplish. I had to make an initial decision and commit to it knowing that something along the way might try to change my mind.

Once my destination and end-game were established in my mind, I had to become self-aware of my current state and make the necessary adjustments to prepare. Although, I was convinced that I would finish the race and receive a medal, the work and preparation became my responsibility. My expectation of being a marathon finisher would not have happened without the help of others. Just like my running group support team, oftentimes you may have to seek the support of other like-minded individuals to help build your courage and keep you inspired to pursue your life's mission.

Finally, it is time to pursue! Once prayer and preparation have taken place, it is time to take the bold step forward. It is in this moment that you are able to run toward your goal confidently knowing that this is your time! It is the courageous act of faith that will drive you in your pursuit. When your preparation meets the right opportunity, you know it is God's timing. Although you may have moments that will try to force you off-course, always take time to recalibrate yourself back to your original purpose.

Overall, what you must understand is that once you are committed to taking ownership and refuse to define your life by temporary setbacks, you are in control of completing your life's goal. You can bounce back from any setback or failure. Sometimes you may actually be the hindrance to accomplishing your own victories. Instead of focusing on what is happening to you, it's time for you to take control and be exceptional.

Remember, this life's journey is more like a marathon than a sprint. When you are more mindful of the small steps, eventually you will build the momentum and the endurance you need to achieve the big goals. The larger goal will not overwhelm you when you are confident in the preparation stage of consistency.

Now get back to life! It's happening as we speak!

Sherrod Schuler is poised, polished, and articulate speaker, presenter of ideas, and leader. He is an accomplished management professional with significant achievements in the financial services industry. Sherrod is an ordained minister with the Jabula New Life International Network and an Associate Pastor of Embassy Covenant Church International of Troy, MI. He received his bachelor's degree from Grand Valley State University and holds an MBA from Spring Arbor University. Sherrod resides in the Metro Detroit area with his wife, Bridgette Schuler. He is the proud father of a remarkable daughter, Autumn.

Website: www.sherrodspeaks.com

Remember Who You Are

By Stacie Winkfield

I could hear my wireless device ringing a notification, and within the seconds it took to open up my email, the entire direction of my weekend and my life shifted. My eyes skimmed the words before me that stated, for only 897 dollars, I could be face to face with one of my she-roes. I couldn't get into my leather phone holder and swipe my credit card quick enough! All I could think of was the huge black check mark I'd be able to mark on my vision board as an accomplishment for that year. In less than 24 hours, I would be face-to-face with a woman who I looked up to for most of my adult life. This year became my personal year of yes. For that accomplishment, I thank Miss Shonda Rhymes. I emerged that year willing to do whatever it took to meet every goal I set for myself. "Whatever it takes," became my mantra along my personal pursuit of happiness.

I left work that day and rushed home to pick my girls up from school. I dropped them off at my mom's house, and then texted their father to tell him where he could pick them up for the weekend. I grabbed as many decent "mom dresses" as I could find, and packed them in my carry-on bag. I had no money for a hotel room, so I planned to wash up in the gas station restroom. I set out alone, driving four hours away from my home towards Chicago, bound for a chance to stand face-to-face with the woman I looked up to, so I could look into her eyes and say thank you for helping in my transformation.

The $897 fee was for a VIP opportunity, to be able to ask a question about my business and receive her one-on-one advice. I had my questions ready before I even closed the car door and hit the highway. Arrangements were made for me to stay with my ex's uncle when I arrived. At this point, it really didn't matter to me where I stayed, all that mattered was I would be able to stand with her.

When, I arrived in Chicago that night, it didn't take long before I realized I was in a dilapidated part of the city. And to make matters worse, my ex fiancé's uncle had a wife, who when her husband wasn't listening, told me that I was not welcome to stay. I sat exhausted in the passenger seat of my vehicle, wondering if I would spend the last of my credit card balance on a hotel room, instead of the consumer bill for that month. I settled into the idea of sleeping in my car in a brightly-lit parking lot. I could roll up a pair of jeans as my pillow and use one of my dresses as a blanket. I was more than okay with this task before me. I decided to run after my dream, because the dream was the only tangible thing I had left burning inside of me, even if that dream involved sleeping in cars along the way.

The next two days went by in a blur. When everyone else broke away for lunch breaks, I knelt on the steps of the church where the event was held, praying and fasting. I stood in line waiting at the end of day one, with no book in my hand, but with my heart beating frantically in my chest. I feared that my mentor would grow tired, and that she would leave before she knew how much she meant to me. However, she was very kind and gracious and warm. She looked into my eyes and said, "You drove all this way, just to have this moment?" Then we hugged, me with the ugliest crying face, then dried our makeup and took a selfie. Meeting her was everything I had imagined. And the next day I would get to be a guest in her personal suite to ask questions about my business.

The next morning, I meditated so hard, I imagined the sky lifting when I opened my eyes. Inside of my spirit I felt a direct connect to the Source. I had a need to make sure I was at church that Sunday, bright and early to get spiritually fed.

There were other women who said they were just going to sleep in, but I could not sleep in, for I was running after my nourishment. That is what starving people do. This moment was not a time for rest, this moment was a wrinkle in time to pick up the pace.

After church that morning, I headed to my car to drive to the hotel where the VIP Day was held. I remember searching for a place to park and calling people I had met during Day One, to let the facilitators know, I was on my way. I carried a pair of boat-neck, camel-colored flats in my bag for times like these. When I finally found a parking place, I took off my heels, threw them in my bag, and rushed through the urine-saturated alley like a model late for a go-see. I rushed to get there as soon as I could only to find out everyone else was waiting. My mentor and her team had not even arrived yet. But I was still relieved to be present.

When the team did arrive, I made sure I was on the elevator first. In the hotel suite, I sat up front and hung onto every single word. And when it was time for my question, I embraced every suggestion and ran with every little thing she gave me. What I wasn't prepared for, was not the sleeping in the car, not the washing up in gas stations, or even the shut-off notice that would be coming in the mail for the utilities bill. What I was not prepared for, was for her to extend an invite to me to join her masterclass network.

Simply put, she gave me the blueprint to accomplish what I had asked, but then she said, "If you want to do it 7-10 years quicker, join my masterclass." She wanted to make sure before we left the room that day, we either had a really solid yes, or a really solid no. And I was torn between both, because my heart had a solid yes, but my bank account was a solid no. I had spent the last of my money, just to be in that room, and at that point I felt like a failure for not having the $40,000 to join.

What do you do when you have you choose between the dream in your spirit and what your perceived reality is up until that point? You break!

When I left the room with the big-game players that day, I felt defeated. I felt both less than and not enough. I wanted to join, but knew I was not ready. I was angry at myself for not being financially responsible, so I could jump at this opportunity. I mean, here I was prepared to sleep in my car if I had to, whatever it took, to get to hug her, to look into her eyes and tell her I loved her for being a part of the change in my life. So whatever bones she threw at me I was willing to receive, except she did not throw us bones. She threw us truth, she threw us graciousness, and she threw us nuggets of great business wisdom. I felt less than, because once I got to the room where masters played, I set myself up with an expectation. And then, something as insignificant as money, stood there as a wedge between birthing my dream and my life of mediocrity. I made these two days about the money, and in that moment, forgot about the experience.

So instead of feeling accomplished, I hurried out of the room as fast as I could, in hope that no one would notice me leaving. When I got to the garage where my car was parked, I sat in the driver's seat bawling like a baby. I remember calling my father and asking him for the money. My father said to me, "Even though she is your mentor, she is not God! The same God that works for her will work for you."

I would be okay, but at that moment I was ungrateful. Even though everyone in that VIP room did not try to belittle me, I couldn't find the courage to forgive myself. For me, not having the money meant I wasn't at my best, I wasn't good enough. And so, I drove away from Chicago, so distraught that I put on a four-hour recording and played it back through my phone's earbuds. I became so distracted and wrapped up in my thoughts, that I drove and I drove, and I drove some more, until I finally realized I had driven four hours in the completely opposite direction of where I was supposed to go.

When I realized my mistake, I was mortified. I had a nine-hour drive ahead of me, and I had to report to work the next morning. It was pitch black outside, one o'clock in the morning, and I was in the middle of nowhere. I still had on my dress from the event earlier, and finally it dawned on me, I had not used the restroom all day. I was so focused on not missing anything, a word that was said, or a beat or a breath in the room that day. I placed everything on the line, including my bladder, which at that very moment felt the need to kick in. I turned the car around on a side street, set my GPS for home, and headed in the opposite direction.

A police officer pulled me over after I started back, for driving slightly over the center line. He gave me a warning after I refused to get out of the car and walk back to his car with him, in case he had any further questions. I knew he was hinting at questioning my sobriety, but I was afraid. I was a woman, alone, in the dark, in my dress, who had not used the restroom all day. I had driven four hours in the wrong direction. I was an emotional wreck. And that last request of the officer was one that I simply could not grant. I stood firmly in my no, and in my head, he would have to drag me out of the window of that car to get me into his vehicle. I was done with everything, the crying, the bargaining with God, the ungratefulness. And then, at that moment I understood why God took me four hours the wrong way.

Our version of the "wrong way" is, at most times, the universe's gentle push into an alternate direction to grow us. A loan refused, a relationship failed, a job we have been relieved of, all experiences to derail us from the straight and narrow path and onto our personal road for greatness. Only in this place do we evaluate our truest potential, use our imagination, and create the possibility of not what's normal, but what's next. A change of course, a dark abandoned road, and four hours in the opposite direction led me to humbleness. Along the long road home, I realized, in more ways than one, that I was in the right place at the right time, and that there were never any mistakes. I let my perception of what should have happened, overshadow all that did happen.

When you look to compare yourself to, stand amongst, or be in connection to others that may not see the dream buried deep within you, remember the words of my father. "Even though they may be great men or women, they are not God. And the same God that worked for them, will work for you."

That day I did not have the $40,000 in cash, but what I did have was 40 million dollars' worth of heart. I took every bit of the advice my mentor gave me and implemented it to the best of my ability to run my business. I admit, I was praying that she would see the greatness in me, that she would look into my face and see the next Bill Gates. I imagined myself cultivating an aura, and glowing like Bruce Leroy from the movie, *The Last Dragon*. I was hoping my mentor would receive the vision in her heart that I prayed for her to see, and offer me her training for free. But that is not how the real world works. The world does not owe me or you anything.

We cannot expect others to see the dream God left budding inside of us. Other people are not responsible for bringing our dreams to fruition. It is up to you to find your burning bud, plant it firmly in good soil, nurture it, water it, and tell it how beautiful it is every day. Speak life into yourself daily, minute by minute. So, when your flower is placed amongst all the other flowers, brightly colored, then and only then can you remember what makes you unique and who you really are.

 Stacie Winkfield is a Licensed Registered Nurse and a Business Branding and Personal Development Coach that teaches her clients unique techniques on how to Break Bravely into their Best Life. She helps her clients go from having an imposter syndrome to showing up as confident world leaders and becoming the brand that everyone loves to follow. As a result of working with her, Stacie's clients are able to move past self-limiting beliefs, create a committed tribe of supporters, and show up in the world as they explore their beauty in ways they could have never imagined.

Stacie is the best-selling author of *Breaking Bravely*. Her greatest joy is seeing lives transformed by the stories of those told around us. Visit her at **www.breakingbravely.com**

Stacie lives with her three children in Michigan, along with her American Eskimo dog P-Jelly, and her committed obsession with movie-theater popcorn.

Find Stacie on Social Media:

https://www.facebook.com/BreakingBravely

Follow her on Instagram @stacie_winkfield

Email her at **MaximizeYourCapacity@gmail.com**

Design Your Life

By Laverne Wyatt

What do Nelson Mandela, graphic design, and Norway have in common? Me. This story will offer an insight into the apartheid regime in South Africa, how graphic design has been used as a tool first to discriminate then later to integrate, and the lessons learned from being a love ex-patriot and single-mom entrepreneur in a country known for Vikings, salmon, and social conformity. I hope that my journey of self-reinvention and rising above my boundaries will help you rise above yours.

Be a troublemaker like Nelson Mandela

"It always seems impossible until it is done." Nelson Mandela

As a 'coloured' child growing up in apartheid South Africa, I had no idea of the spiritual and political fight Mandela endured for us, for our freedom to love, learn, and live where we wanted. Not many know, but Nelson Mandela's forename, *Rolihlahla*, is a Xhosa term colloquially meaning "troublemaker," and as a black female and now entrepreneur expat in Norway, I found myself relating to the term.

Nelson Mandela was born in Mthatha, the same area of the South Africa that both sides of my family originate from. In the 1800's, German and Irish missionaries settled there to spread the word of God and their seed to the local Xhosa population, - which led to me appearing mixed due to my illegal Xhosa and

European heritage. This heritage I passed on to my Norwegian children today.

Besides being a mother of two young boys, democracy and design became two very important themes in my life.

"There is no passion to be found playing small in settling for a life that is less than the one you are capable of living." Nelson Mandela

This beach is for whites only

As a young child, my most memorable experience with graphic design was of having to walk past a beach whose official signage stated, "This beach is for whites only." During apartheid there always seemed to be a sign or paperwork telling us where we should not be, and what we could not do. Even the design of the roads, houses, and communities we lived in were created to divide ethnic groups, to control, and to officially restrict movement of people, money, and opportunities of those not born or classified as 'white.' As a designer today, I feel anger towards the power of a profession I love so much, to affect the lives of so many in that way. I also feel a responsibility to use design to empower and integrate those who feel restricted.

But, can you eat design?

Design was not for black people. My school did not offer Art in any way or form. Design and Art were 'white people' professions; they created the 'formal' communication we consumed and we created the 'informal' crafts, music, and designs that were shared amongst us. We had no examples of any person of colour as a role model in the formal design and advertising sector. Most design did not even show people who looked like us. If one wanted to be an artist, we also did a great job of holding each other back, saying things like, "How can you be an artist? Can you eat art for dinner? Will that pay your rent?"

"Education is the most powerful weapon which you can use to change the world." Nelson Mandela

The mother that never gave up until her daughter became a designer

My mother was the manager of a jewellery store, and employed one the first 'white' people I ever had the chance to hold a long conversation with in my life. I was 17 years old. He advised my mother of a design course that would give me a one-year introduction to a variety of design disciplines. I remember the financial sacrifices my family made that year to pay for my educational fees. That year, the college experienced the first wave of black students who were now finally allowed to study at a higher institution. I was one of two non-white females in the class, attending with students who had studied art all throughout school, with new names of artists and places I had never heard of. I felt so stupid, yet so inspired to be learning something I had loved all my life. I graduated top of my class. Eight years later, I became one of the first waves of black female Art Directors at a top advertising agency in Durban. I helped create the formal communication I always dreamt of. And at that time, I met my Norwegian husband and moved abroad.

"I am the master of my fate: I am the captain of my soul." Nelson Mandela

The grass is always greener in Norway – or is it?

I had met the man of my dreams, who was enlightened enough to see me for who I was and more. We settled into being the happy, hipster couple in the most multi-cultural neighbourhood in downtown Oslo for a while, before moving to the countryside. Career-wise though, my 10 years of work experience in design and perfect English did NOT get me a permanent job in design for at least five years, though we assumed it would, and we struggled. I was shocked. What was going on?

At every turn I felt I my abilities were underestimated, because suddenly I was not just South African, but African. For the first time I was not Laverne, but rather a black woman from Africa, experiencing the stigma of a starving, tragic people that years of media pumped into a society, through one-sided news reporting. My confidence and identity took a dive.

Again, I experienced design and advertising that reflected only a part of society. Where were the people that looked like me? We had two children, mixed as well. Where were their role models? These questions bubbled under the surface as I tried to keep my head, working as a freelancer in advertising for musicians and organisations in the cultural sector.

I experienced hurdle after hurdle. I learned the language, eventually had to work for free to get a job and prove I could actually design.

"It is what we make out of what we have given, not what we are given, that separates one person from another." Nelson Mandela

How do you accept that a marriage is ending and that you can never move back home with your kids?

There is no worse impression than feeling that you are in a life situation that you cannot change. It is like a jail sentence that follows you everywhere you go. I felt unhappy that I was not fulfilling my life in the creative and expansive way that I felt I was meant to and angry about being a divorce statistic. I loved the safety, the courteousness of the Norwegian people and country, and the friends I made there. I worked with a lovely group of people at a medium-sized Norwegian advertising agency and appreciated the stability and support it provided. At the same time, I felt I had to curb my enthusiasm, direct opinions, self-expression, and personality to fit a society that believed in sameness and *'janteloven.'* The rules of society that state:

> You're not to think *you* are anything special.
>
> You're not to think *you* are as good as *we* are.
>
> You're not to think *you* are smarter than *we* are.
>
> You're not to imagine *yourself* better than *we* are.
>
> You're not to think *you* know more than *we* do.
>
> You're not to think *you* are more important than *we* are.
>
> You're not to think *you* are good at anything.
>
> You're not to laugh at *us*.
>
> You're not to think anyone cares about *you*.
>
> You're not to think *you* can teach *us* anything.

The advice of a cherished Norwegian client was for me to throw the rule book out the window and rise above the fear. I chose to do three of the riskiest things in my life - ever. I ended my marriage, began raising our kids in a shared parenting agreement that worked out well, and left the job I worked for five years to get - with no financial backup.

Why? Because I realised that there were so many talented, experienced people from all over the world moving to Norway who had trouble integrating and promoting their talents enough to earn a living from it. Our stories were not told in the media, instead stories of refugees and the strain it provides on society were constant headliners.

"For to be free is not merely to cast off one's chains, but to live in a way that respects and enhances the freedom of others."
Nelson Mandela

The alchemy of turning Pain to Profit

As a designer I needed to help uplift and motivate people who felt marginalised based on their cultural differences. Those people, who dared to break those 10 societal *Janteloven* rules, needed the help of someone who believed in the power of design to empower them to be seen, heard, and counted in society in a positive manner.

There are thousands of Eastern Europeans, Africans, Asians, and Americans all living and working in Europe who need to be counted and seen in the media. They need to have access to the power of creativity and design to help them integrate and express who they really are. I started my own company, with the help of an investor (The law of attraction!), and now run workshops all over Scandinavia, teaching the tips and tricks of design to people who want to feel free to take their life in the direction they feel it should go in.

It is a tough journey which is exciting and allows me to feel free and empowered again. I am now happy to be living here in Norway, and raising my kids on a piece of land that requires constant attention by me, a woman who grew up in the ghetto and suburbs of Durban, South Africa.

I embrace the fact that I am not the social norm, that my experiences of discrimination in South Africa and also the love of my family and community have given me the strength to go beyond psychological and physical borders today. I am also grateful for Norwegian society's support of Nelson Mandela and the anti-apartheid movement which eventually helped fund my freedom.

Today I run one of the only media agencies made up a team of only foreigners in Norway. We hail from five different countries, speaking a total of six languages, and are dedicated to helping people who feel isolated with their great ideas to integrate and succeed in Norway. We develop design and promotional concepts for Norwegian organisations and companies embracing the multicultural reality of society today and are constantly turning our challenges and pain into profit.

"There is no passion to be found playing small - in settling for a life that is less than the one you are capable of living."
Nelson Mandela

Laverne Wyatt is a Design Doctor, Design Advisor, and Entrepreneur who has designed for international and national brands, as well as the local cultural sector. She is a 37-year-old single mom of two Norwegian boys (7 and 3 years old). Laverne is from South Africa and was in the first wave of black women to work in Advertising after the fall of apartheid. She lives on her farm in Halden, Norway and in the capital, Oslo. Her experience from working in Durban, Malta, Norway, and Sweden doing graphic design, fashion design, teaching, event organising, and running workshops has made her an expert in cross-cultural communication and design.

Find out more about Laverne and her work at:
Laverne@inlivingcolourmedia.com

"It always seems impossible until it is done." Nelson Mandela

Business and Relationships Built on the Rock

By Dr. Emmanuel Nwoye

Spiritual Prosperity vs. Wealth

A man is happy if he is wealthy.

Is this a true statement?

No. This statement is absolutely false, spiritually. The wealth of a man does not consist of his possessions but on his richness towards God.

Recently, a friend of mine, Mr. Smith referred his friend, Jerry (not their real names) in order for me to help resolve his business and family problems.

After exchanging pleasantries, I asked Jerry deep searching questions to establish who he was. I started our conversation, "Jerry, tell me everything that I need to know about you and your business."

He appeared very relaxed and emptied himself to enable me to pick and choose whatever information that I needed to help him.

His manifesting problems were that he couldn't sleep more than four hours at nights, and even those four hours were mostly shallow. His doctors had tried to help him for two years before giving up and placing him on sleeping tablets.

His business practices were very good; he treated his employees well. Yet, his business lost profits three years in a row, and one of his employees had quit the previous week.

He was still financially comfortable, but his marriage was under strain because their two teenage children were having problems. His son was on drugs and his daughter wasn't doing well at school.

Jerry went to church once in a while but hadn't yet come to grips with the concept of total forgiveness of his enemies.

Being a Christian coach with a business background, when I got to "forgiveness" I stopped digging deeper into Jerry's troubles. I found the key that I needed to unlock the problems that I recognized in his life.

Jerry was living under stress, fear, and insecurity. Yet, I noticed that as I asked searching questions, Jerry warmed up to me, indicating that he had hope in my process, because my probing, though intrusive, was partnered to his problems.

Factoring God into Business

I told Jerry that he had two choices: the pursuit of wealth or pursuit of prosperity. I knew both options were efforts to achieving happiness. But I don't usually advise clients on how to get wealth; instead, I advise them on how to become 'spiritually prosperous.'

Spiritual prosperity virtually guarantees lasting happiness, and in many cases leads to wealth also.

Both Jerry and I agreed that his family needed to be grounded in Christ, and to live the life of believers. When that step was done, he would have the right foundation on which to build his business. His children would make the right decisions in life and the right selection of their own spouses.

Believing, Forgiveness, and Obedience

If you believe in Jesus Christ as your personal Savior, you become a child of God; a Prince. As a child of God, it is mandatory that you totally forgive all the people who offended you before you ask God to forgive your own sins.

Total forgiveness is difficult to understand and even more difficult to implement. But I will unpack the concept of forgiveness in such a way that you will understand it clearly, to the extent that you shall become fearful for not forgiving as commanded by God.

Forgiveness is the only key to spiritual prosperity. It is also the only door that leads you to your 'place of rest,' which is that time and place in your life when all your enemies are defeated, and you are living the purpose in life for which God created you.

From that point, you can begin to factor God into your business and life decisions.

However, if you don't forgive others, God cannot forgive you and you can't become a heavenly Prince. Instead, you shall harbor vengeful demonic spirits that attract evil and bad luck to you and your business from time to time.

You are, in effect, robbing God of what belongs to Him. He said, "Vengeance is mine." Yet, you refuse to let go of the thoughts and the pains that your offender inflicted on you. As a result, you inadvertently continue to wish the person misfortunes because of what he did to you. So, don't play God. Just forgive; whether the person repents or not is immaterial.

When you accept the importance of forgiveness, you must then take your relationship with the Lord to the next level, your 'place of rest'. Your 'place of rest' is when your pursuit of life is in keeping with God's purpose for you. You can then ask for anything in the name of Jesus, and it shall be given to you.

I had very good results in my MBA and performed very well at managerial level for my employers. My greatest strengths are developing and motivating the people who work for me.

But I don't coach anybody in business until that person has mastered how to factor God into his life. In other words, I don't give fish to people; instead, I give them nets so that they don't come back to me again for fish unless they want to buy more nets. I simply give them the tools to master their own life.

So, Jerry agreed to get his business, his marriage, and his family in line with God's instructions so they could resonate like a symphony where the Holy Spirit is the Conductor. Using God's ways, the home provides a nest to roost after a long day's work, business brings the money to pay the bills, and children, while supported by their parents, learn how to cope with the world.

I had to explain total forgiveness further to ensure that Jerry was as passionate about it as I am.

The key to this concept is to finally realize that your enemy is more valuable to you than a gold nugget. Your best friend may fellowship with you, lend you money, offer you a shoulder to cry on, give you advice that can grow you in wisdom, including spiritually. You trust him and would do the same things for him.

However, in the case of your worst enemy, using God's laws to overcome the period of your enemy's torment, will allow you to receive a 'well-done' pat on the back from God. God will trust you more and give you higher responsibilities in your purpose for Him.

When God allowed Satan to test you for spiritual promotion, your enemy acted as the catalyst for your test. His actions allowed you to grow spiritually. It is as if he knelt on all fours and let you step on him in order to collect your victory from a high shelf!

Without your enemy as a vessel that Satan used to challenge you, the test would have never started, and your spiritual advancement would not have been achieved.

That promotion is why God commands you to love your enemy and pray for him because your enemy does not know what he is doing. So, obey God and ask Him to help you throughout the testing period.

After obeying and passing the test, you will get a very rare sense of victory, joy, and peace of mind that money can't buy. Even some of your friends will begin to notice a glow on your face, confirming that you are a happy man.

Never forget that loving and praying for your enemy are the keys to total forgiveness.

Having achieved total forgiveness, you are then equipped with your personal testimony that you can use to counsel and coach your children and other friends in similar tests of life. You shall become more credible if you are able to say, "I was once there."

Encounter with God

You deserve congratulations when you get to this point and still believe that these actions will work.

The next step towards linking your new belief systems to your business is to wrestle with God.

In your persistent prayer, ask God to reveal to you why you were created, and let Him tell you what you should be doing on earth at this moment of your life. Be warned; this prayer is a dangerous gamble, because the answer may require that you make a drastic economic change in your business, move to another country, etc. Yet, it may also turn out that you are already on the correct route, or can continue and join the correct route later.

Through this prayer, you ask God for a life navigation tool that I call "GPS," an acronym for God's Positioning System. God will show you His purpose for your life and put you in your 'place of rest.'

The transition may be instant or may take months, if not years. But the good news is that you are on a journey in which you can fulfill God's plan for you, the course that leads to the God-planned finish line for you.

You must thank God for whatever outcome that you receive. The concept of God's positioning is not only applicable to business but to all aspects of your life, including marriage, employment, personal development, travels, etc.

The Finish Line

When I convinced Jerry to trust my coaching and to love and pray for his enemies, I noticed him heave a great sigh of relief. I knew right away that I got my man, through the power of the Holy Spirit. Then it was time to rub in the process so that he would be able to not only be happy now but also to finish life well.

I asked for his phone number and texted him a message that a friend sent to me a few months previously. I found the text useful in explaining to people what they could expect on their deathbed.

Life is like a race and a deathbed is like a finish line. Most athletes have optimal race plans that they follow to ensure a happy ending; a win. The race of life should end happily in victory as well.

Since I am unaware of the story's origin, I changed the name of the author.

"On the sick bed -- Mark Jacobs' Last Words -

I reached the pinnacle of success in the business world.

In others' eyes, my life is an epitome of success.

However, aside from work, I have little joy. In the end, wealth is only a fact of life that I am accustomed to.

At this moment, lying on the sick bed and recalling my whole life, I realize that all the recognition and wealth that I took so much pride in, have paled and become meaningless in the face of impending death.

You can employ someone to drive the car for you, make money for you, but you cannot have someone to bear the sickness for you.

Material things lost can be found. But there is one thing that can never be found when it is lost – Life.

When a person goes into the operating room, he will realize that there is one book that he has yet finished reading – "The Book of a Healthy Life."

Whichever stage in life we are at right now, with time, we will face the day when the curtain comes down.

Treasure love for your family, love for your spouse, love for your friends...

Treat yourself well. Cherish others.

As we grow older and hence wiser, we slowly realize that wearing a $300 or $30 watch - - - they both tell the same time;

Whether we carry a $300 or $30 wallet or handbag - - - the amount of money inside is the same;

Whether we drink a bottle of $300 or $10 wine - - - the hangover is the same;

Whether the house we live in is 300 or 3000 square feet - - - loneliness is the same.

You will realize, your true inner happiness does not come from the material things of this world.

Whether you fly first or economy class, if the plane goes down - - -you go down with it...

Therefore, I hope you realize when you have mates, buddies, and old friends, brothers, and sisters, who you chat with, laugh with, talk with, sing songs with, talk about north-south-east-west, or heaven and earth ... That is true happiness!!"

This testimony is a good philosophy of life because the assessment of a man's life at his deathbed, as successful, is preferred to an assessment of being a failure at the death bed, no matter how well one lived.

The philosophy is in agreement with mine because I pursue a lifestyle that aims to achieve a happy deathbed ending.

Other philosophies in the pursuit of wealth may earn you millions of dollars, but do not guarantee happiness.

God guarantees His children a roof over their heads, food on their tables, and raiment over their bodies. This assurance is called spiritual prosperity, and it creates happiness continuously.

When I was translated to Paradise in February 2013, for about 35 minutes, I lost all earthly emotions completely. While I was there, I didn't remember that there was a place called Earth; I forgot my family and my job.

My new reality then was in the company of many millions of other redeemed believers who were standing asleep and waiting for the trumpet to sound from the "Kingdom City" situated over 50 miles away from where I stood.

The thrill, that I experienced, which I had no words to describe, flowed through my body continuously.

That was the true happiness a man gets at the end of his life by living God's purpose for Him.

Every other pursuit is an effort in futility.

Dr. Emmanuel Nwoye coaches and counsels people from their point of desperation into highly motivated, spiritually prosperous individuals. His clients quickly learn how to factor God into their business to attain spiritual prosperity using God's plan for their lives. Using his tested triangular model for spouse selection, woven around BABs, (Behavior, Attitude, and Belief-systems) he coaches his clients to make virtually divorce-proof choices for their spouses. This powerful spouse-selection model also shows how to fix faltering marriages. He believes that wealth may lead to depression and that spiritual prosperity, which oftentimes includes wealth, leads to happiness and peace of mind.

He uses his spiritual gifts of prophecy, healing, and the blessing he received during a translation to Paradise in 2013 to show his clients God's easier and safer way of living.

Born to a poor Christian family in Nigeria, God helped Emmanuel to earn his Master of Business Administration and Hon. Ph.D. in Christian Ministries, from American universities. After working in senior management for two American organizations, he had a calling to end his third working career driving trains. He thereafter went to the International Bible Institute of London for his Diploma in Christian Ministries.

He has been married for 42 years to his wife Iffy; and has four children, Andy, Marylee, Maxine, and Marlene, all happily married, and six grandchildren.

Contact Emmanuel on his website http://SpiritualProsperityNow.com as well as on YouTube, Facebook, Linkedin, Google, and Twitter.

Wisdom of the Creek

By Lisa Nielsen

To everything there is a season, and a time to every purpose under the heaven. Ecclesiastes 3:1

A creek isn't a mighty river. Nor is it a babbling brook. The goal of the creek is to get water from one place to another. It's simple. The creek takes water from a babbling brook and deposits it into a river where it can continue on. A simple, clean task. From a distance the creek looks simple.

I grew up living beside my creek. I loved to wander along the slippery bank that was overgrown with bushes and trees. If I started at the bridge, I would be limited to only the area where most kids played. I preferred to start below my house. Most of the creek had a slippery bank, overgrown and a little dangerous for entering the water. There was a foundation and fireplace of a long-gone house that still remained next to the creek. I walked down the sloping steps and perched on the last one to watch the rushing water bounce over the rocks. Trees grew abundantly along the creek. Often the water eroded the soil from the roots. The trees fell and sometimes created a bridge. The water was usually fast right there, and most kids left that place alone. The creek was well-known, and many kids liked to play in it. But most of the time, I had it to myself.

It occurred to me that this creek was more complicated than water rushing from one place to another. It was required to find its way around many rocks, trees, trails, hills, and a myriad of other natural obstacles. The creek designed its own path. At some places, it spread out and became calmer. In other places it was deep and rushing. Because the creek flowed through people's yards and lives, often the creek required the help of humans to maintain its banks. The creek was a familiar unknown in my life. It was a calming influence, and I modeled much of my life around the natural ways of the creek. In calm times I realize it helps to be prepared for whatever comes next. Not knowing what challenges are around the next corner, it is a good idea to listen and watch carefully for any signs of trouble. Like the creek, it seems I have followed my own path. I found my way around obstacles. Sometimes they were obstacles I created by my own choices. I made mistakes at work, at school, in raising my children, and in dealing with a disabled spouse. Finding a solution to the problems my mistakes created has been challenging for me. I learned to dig deep inside myself for a solution. It has helped me be humble in asking for assistance, and to appreciate the people who are willing to help me. Sometimes the obstacles weren't of my own doing. Those obstacles were sometimes created by family members, co-workers, or friends. This type of challenge seems to be simpler for me to find a resolution. Perhaps it's because I didn't cause the trouble. If I wasn't the cause of the problem, I don't have any emotional ties to it and my perspective comes from a different angle. Like the creek, sometimes it takes a bit of work to resolve a problem, and sometimes it's a simple solution.

In the winter, the creek's banks were frozen and dangerous. The snow and ice were treacherous and unforgiving. One misstep could mean an entire ski season with a broken leg, or worse. Those times were ones of cautious approach. I stayed further away. Dressing warmly and not approaching the bank at all was a good way to stay out of danger. Watching from a safe distance I observed the icy creek. Angrily the water splashed onto the fallen trees and made an icy bridge. When the sun was out the ice crystals shimmered in the light and danced across the foliage. There were times in the winter when the ice and frost created a mystical fairyland where my young imagination flourished and grew. During these times it occurred to me that being structured and rigid has its place in business and personal matters. Letting people know what to expect, and the limits I have are essential for setting into place. These limits are as important as knowing consequences. Like the beautiful, icy fairyland the creek created, I found it possible to create a family and business that run smoothly by staying firm in the rules that are put in place by experience and wisdom. Reflecting on my mistakes seems to be my best way to develop reasonable rules.

I loved the winter at the creek. Its cold, bleak attitude and seemingly frozen life teemed with activity. Under the frozen trees, the creek still rushed on its way. This was the time when the larger boulders would be ripped loose and tossed into the water, changing the path of the creek. I often chuckled in the spring when I heard comments about the changes that happened. I wondered how people couldn't know that the creek was busy all winter with its housekeeping. I felt winter was a refreshing season, with changes and new places to explore. I learned a lesson in the winters by the creek. I learned that if you have a little bad attitude, and do some cleaning when you are alone, you get a fresher start again. After the bleak, cold necessity of setting rules and laying down limits, the creek taught me take out unneeded boulders that were in the way of the progress needed to further the good of my family and my business.

Spring was full of changes by the creek. There was often a mix of winter and spring, as if the creek would get confused about what season it was. The melting snow created a creek that burst over its banks. Overfilled with water, it would often toss extra boulders and trees into the rushing, swirling water. I felt as if I had new gifts from the mountains in the form of stepping stones and tree bridges. All of these gifts were the result of an overflowing creek. The early spring was the best part of the clean-up and refreshing of the creek. She would get an entire facelift from the extra gifts from the mountains.

The spring was also a time to be wary of animals stretching in the cool spring sun. After a long winter, they loved to race along the new tree bridges and make new homes, never taking note of the human watching them. Baby animals were born. Older animals died during the winter. The cycle continued with or without me. I noticed at times, when baby animals tried to leave their parents too soon, they would perish. Either by starving, or getting too cold, or not being able to defend themselves, they would be trampled by the living of the other animals. I tried to help these unfortunate critters. Sometimes they were so young, I didn't know what sort of animal it was. Could it be a baby squirrel or rat? I would feed the tiny creature until it either died, or lived. Then I would set it out on its own, hoping it could live beyond this first year. There were a lot of little graves dug by the side of the creek. Graves of animals that didn't make it through the winter.

I learned many lessons from the creek in the spring. The first one is that it's just fine if you feel it's not the season for something to happen. Birth, death, and all the steps along life happen. Some are happy, and some sad, but they are never exactly the same. If a life event happens, acknowledge it. Either grieve the event or enjoy it. It may never come around again. Like moss growing on rocks, some events are hard to grasp at first. You may slip and fall on the mossy stones. Events like learning to deal with conflicts with friends, co-workers, and family can all be slippery, mossy stones. You may have many victories crossing the creek successfully without getting wet. Like those victories, it's a happy day when events are smooth.

With perseverance it's possible to work your way through many of life's most cherished times. Events may seem out of place, or slippery, in life, but often, with a little ingenuity and a lot of work, things turn around in the most glorious way possible. It all seems to be determined by experience, wisdom, courage, and a bit of luck.

As spring's turbulent run-off calmed to a summer flow, it was time to enjoy the creek. To immerse myself in her happy, playful attitude. Summer days were full of running along her banks. Building huts in the sunny openings of the creek side. Sleeping under the stars. My favorite sound was to hear the creek. The creek seemed to be busier than normal. Summer thunder storms provided extra water to deal with. Animals were busy with their work. Destruction would flare. If the cause of the destruction was human, animal, or nature-caused, it was the same result. The culprits were found and dealt with, usually by the creek. After the creek dealt with the misbehavior, it was satisfied. If there was a fire, the creek would simply extinguish it. Often the banks of the creek would cave in, either from children playing or erosion. The creek would soothe the wounds and smooth out the rough spots. Sometimes the rough spots became an extra turn or small water fall. The creek remembered the changes made to its banks and creek bed. Always adapting and changing, the creek was satisfied and went back to its slower summer attitude. In my life, I've learned to remember the offenses that are done to me, but forgive, and go on. It's not worth holding a grudge. I feel if an offense has happened, it might take a lot of work to smooth it down to a manageable event, but it's worth doing. My world seems to run more calmly if I can work with the erosion and damage done. I can adapt to changes and keep flowing like the creek.

Summers offered a time of playfulness and rejoicing. It was common to grab a tube to float on, and ride from one spot to another spot without stopping. The banks looked different from the view on the creek. I noticed the rocks hiding under the washed-out banks. The animals were often less aware of me as I quietly floated down the creek, and the sky seemed even more blue. The creek hid treats for those who were willing to make an extra effort to explore. I could understand why the bank would break away from itself if I viewed it from the creek. Insights are often gained by taking a different view, or looking through someone else's eyes. In life, your view of an event is much different than other people's views. Putting yourself in your child's or an employee's position will offer new explanations and perspectives. Compassion, understanding, and wisdom often follow a new perspective.

Fall was a beautiful time at the creek. Foliage slowed its growth. The creek whisked away the falling leaves and brush. It was possible to clearly see the other side of the bank. The creek knew the fall would turn to winter, and enjoyed this time of quiet reflection. The animals busied themselves with making sure they had food and a warm home to spend the winter in. For me, I loved to spend time reading near the bank of the creek, taking in the scent of decaying leaves. Fall was a quiet time on the creek. The creek didn't have as much water, and delightfully bounced over rocks. The low water created pools that would reflect a wavy image back to me. Reflecting on the things we learn is a good exercise in patience, kindness, and understanding of what others are experiencing. Remembering the ups and downs in life is an important way of discovering improvements I can make. At home, work, or wherever I am, I feel I'm a better person if I can better myself by remembering important lessons I've learned.

As I reflect on what I've learned from the creek, I realize there are many more lessons to learn. Lessons of perseverance, abundance, lack, and simply flowing along.

Lisa B. Nielsen was born and raised in Salt Lake City, Utah. She attended Southern Utah State College where she met and married her sweetheart, Jim Nielsen. They spent 13 years raising 3 beautiful children together. In 1991, Jim survived a massive stroke which he courageously survived. This stroke provided an opportunity to grow further than Lisa thought possible. For the next 25 years, Lisa was Jim's caregiver. Learning, compassion, patience, and business skills were her focus.

During the years when her children were small, Lisa spent many years working for a clinical laboratory, then eventually migrated into an Insurance supplement career, which she loves. In addition to her insurance business, Lisa is an advocate for disabled adults.

Lisa loves to travel, and is within reach of her life-long goal of visiting every state in the United States of America. She also loves to sing, and has performed with a community choir for most of the last 18 years.

Lisa is the mother of 3 adult children, and the grandmother of 11 grandchildren. She loves family life, and strives to stay close to her family.

She is thankful for the unwanted trials, where she feels she has learned the biggest lessons in her life. These lessons bring her closer to the Lord, her family, and her core beliefs.

She can be contacted at lisanielsen01@gmail.com

Not Good Enough to Live, Too Good to Die

By Sandra Stachowicz

The turning point in my life came about four years ago. I was kicked out of my home, my long-term relationship broke up, and I was laid off from my job. I developed breathing difficulties, suffered from insomnia, and eventually became depressed. Sometimes I even thought I'd like to 'check out.'

It all happened within only six months!

To top it all off, I contracted a debilitating and potentially life-threatening illness. I was in a lot of pain and my feet were so swollen I could not walk! I hung onto my bed's metal frame to soothe my feverish body. My body was on fire!

I hit rock bottom when I was forced to crawl on the apartment floor just to get to the toilet.

My mind played tricks on me, "Is this IT?! Am I dying?!" I was not ready to die! I felt like I hadn't truly lived yet! Worse yet, I had no idea what was going on with me! It felt as if my body was shutting down on me. LIFE was shutting down on me.

Out of desperation I turned to my landlord asking for help getting to the hospital. He declined citing health concerns.

It was raining cats and dogs. My feet were so swollen that none of my shoes fit any more. All of a sudden, the few steps down the staircase seemed insurmountable. Every step I took to get into a taxi caused excruciating pain.

I ended up being rushed to the hospital.

The hospital refused to take me in as their in-patient, claiming there was nothing they could do for me. So instead, they sent me back home to fend for myself. "How could they?!" I thought to myself. I could barely walk, let alone feed myself!

I desperately cried for help, yet felt completely alone and isolated. I couldn't even leave my flat to get groceries! I ended up eating whatever scraps of food I could get my hands on.

I was under quarantine for a month. Worse yet, none of my family visited me during that time.

Then my boyfriend magically 'disappeared' from my life at the time when I needed him most! I felt lonely, abandoned, and betrayed. I was dealing with an avalanche of physical and emotional pain. That's when the moment of clarity came:

"THERE'S A REASON FOR ALL THIS SUFFERING. I DON'T KNOW WHAT IT IS YET, BUT I AM GOING TO FIND OUT!"

I just wished the reason would hurry up and make itself known! I was sick and tired of feeling like I wasn't good enough! Not good enough to live, too good to die! I tried to be happy, but when I looked at my current situation, I asked myself, "How did I end up here?"

Unable to move or leave my flat, the only thing that kept me going was sensing my Dad's spirit. When I was fifteen years old, my beloved father suddenly passed away after a heart-attack. But, confined to my bed, I could FEEL his presence, yet couldn't quite put words to it.

His love encompassed me and gave me the courage to continue when the going got too tough for me to take. It was my Dad's love that gave me the much-needed strength, when everything else failed.

On the surface it looked like my life was reduced to crumbs practically overnight, but the REAL reason my life fell apart is because it was never whole to begin with.

I felt deserted by the people closest to me. Only this time, the people who abandoned me were still alive. I couldn't help but feel like that little girl again abandoned by her father.

My dad had no life insurance or savings that could support my widowed mother or her five daughters. For several months we relied heavily on our family and community support, and for many years my mother struggled to put food on our table. While I certainly was devastated my father was not around, in many ways I felt my life was easier, because with little or no choice left, I suddenly stopped being an innocent child and turned into a young woman. I understood from an early age, that rather than leaving anything to chance, I had to take control of my life.

Life was a struggle even before my dad's spiritual contract ran its course. Life went from dark to pitch black. I couldn't help but believed that the people I loved either died, abandoned me, or were never there to begin with, like my emotionally cold mother, who I felt I never REALLY had.

Losing her beloved husband took a toll on my mother's health, and after my Dad's sudden departure she suffered a nervous breakdown. My mother confessed she didn't want us kids, and the only reason she had us was because our father wanted to. I grew up feeling ignored, unheard, and criticized at every turn. This in turn made me feel like I was not allowed to just feel what I was feeling or say what I needed to say. I felt like I had no voice. I felt like I didn't deserve to be there. I thought terrible thoughts about myself and my life that left me feeling like there was something FUNDAMENTALLY wrong with me!

This feeling wasn't just a question of low self-esteem, but something more profound. I concluded that I was lacking, worthless, and unlovable.

I desperately sought my mother's love, yet was afraid of the consequences of seeking it. I mourned the mother I needed, wanted, and deep down felt I deserved, yet never REALLY possessed. I mourned my Dad's premature and senseless death, but the voice echoing in my head was my mum's, telling me what I wasn't — smart, beautiful, kind, loving, worthy.

My soul would die a little every time my mother made a nasty remark about everything I WASN'T.

Deep down, I knew I was NOT my circumstances or the voice in my head. I knew I was meant for MORE!

So, at the age of 19, I decided that enough was enough. I bought a one-way ticket and moved from a small village in Poland, to the bustling city of Edinburgh, to chase down my passion like it was the last bus of the night. My hope was that moving to a different country would give me a fresh start and make me stop feeling worthless, lacking, and unlovable.

I could hardly understand the Scottish accent, so I had to draw on my true strength to find work in a foreign country where I knew no one.

Despite just wanting to give up, I stayed in Edinburgh because I just knew that this little stubborn girl was supposed to do something BIG across the continent. My soul was definitely calling me at that time.

Ironically, I thought that getting a good degree from a prestigious university abroad would be the key to success. I managed multi-million-pound projects by the age of 26, and my job made me feel important (at least on paper!) yet I couldn't help but feel like I was fooling people, fearing I would be found out when I enjoyed success in the world. I soon realised, that sitting in an office all day and spending four hours a day commuting to work, was not my path. So, I took a leap of faith, left my big corporate job and embarked on an entrepreneurial journey.

After qualifying as a massage therapist, I moved back to Scotland, naïve in my thinking that money would bring happiness! Not surprisingly, my first business attempt failed, and I ended up getting a menial job addressing letters 40 hours a week. With each letter I addressed, I felt like my soul was dying a slow and painful death. I knew I had to do something!

An opportunity presented itself after my sister introduced me to online marketing, and I launched my second business. Unbeknownst to me, I entered a whole new territory, the world of possibilities, the world where everything was possible, the land of promise – the world of personal development. But it wasn't until I was confined to my bed and feared for my life that I completely threw myself into personal development. I read every book out there, immersed myself in every self-growth course I could get my hands on and as soon as I got back on my feet I attended every seminar!

I felt like these personal development leaders were speaking my language, and it was only then that I felt like I had FINALLY come home! For the first time in my life I felt understood. But, still I felt like I was spinning my wheels and repeating patterns in my life. I had trouble asking for what I really needed and wanted. I had difficulty setting healthy boundaries. I listened to what everyone else said and lost myself along the way. I felt the need to hide and had an inability to sell myself or my work. I desperately wanted to break out of the patterns running (and ruining) my life, but no matter what I did or how hard I tried, I just never seemed to be enough!

I felt like someone or something was holding me back.

It wasn't until much later that I realised that the reason nothing worked to end my struggle up to that point, was because I did not actually have a relationship with myself – I had a relationship with my limiting beliefs!

I bought into the illusion that there was something wrong with me that showed up in my life as a result of my past experiences. It's not that I wasn't good enough, it's that I BELIEVED that I wasn't good enough! The belief was wrong, NOT me!

Once I knew what the culprit was, I still did not know how to break out of those limiting beliefs! I kept coming up to the same blocks, time and time again. The only thing that changed were the people, the circumstances, or the events involved. Essentially, I had that Groundhog Day experience, day-in and day-out!

Not good enough was part of my resume…

When I was a teenager, my mother held me back by focusing on my flaws and imperfections, never my accomplishments. It was only when I was in an emotionally abusive relationship with a man who disappeared on me as I fought for my life, that

I realized that I limited myself, by adopting my mother's view of me in the world.

I unintentionally replicated the relationship I had with my mother. Essentially, I was not in a relationship with my boyfriend, but rather my mother! When I first met him, he was charming and attentive but, in the end, he was like my mother, indifferent and judgemental by turns, hypercritical and passive-aggressive.

When my boyfriend left I realised that I would just never be 'enough' for some people, and most importantly, that someone else's opinion of me does not have to become my reality! Other people can't add or take anything away from me! I ended up 'divorcing' both my boyfriend and my mother.

Changes certainly didn't happen overnight.

When I started my second business, I spent a few years trying to bend myself into the shape I thought others wanted me to buy into. As a result, I forgot what it was that made me, ME. Instead, I fell into the trap of self-criticism, thinly disguised as perfectionism that left me feeling worthless.

I used to think that to make money, I'd have to become someone I wasn't. Now, I know being myself was MORE than enough. It always is!

It wasn't until I was divinely guided to my own high-level coach that I opened my eyes to what I have always been. As a result, I stopped berating myself over everything that I wasn't, and instead I started loving myself for everything that I already was and for everything I was about to become. It's almost as if someone turned on the light switch and illuminated what has ALWAYS been there!

In a sense, my life falling apart was the most beautiful moment ever because it meant I could arrange all the pieces the way I wanted them to.

It was a slow and long journey of self-discovery. There were moments when I wanted to throw in the towel, curl up on a sofa, and simply cry. But I persevered. I survived. I forgave myself and others. I healed. I became.

It is in our darkest moments that we discover our true strength that can never, ever be taken away from us. You can either let it crush your soul, or turn your pain into greatness. I know what it feels like to believe you're not good enough, to feel broken, lacking, worthless, or unlovable. I have walked in your shoes and have come out on the other side!

As women, we often give our power away to people or circumstances outside our control. It's time you OWNED your power! Allow your pain to become your greatest strength. Stop seeking approval and validation from others. Stop asking for permission to be happy. Stop waiting for changes, and instead, BE the change you've been waiting for! Know that the only person who'll ultimately make you happy is the person in the mirror.

As soon as I embraced that truth, the trajectory of my life changed forever.

Almost ten years later, I am here, with a weird hybrid Polish/Scottish accent and a business I love. I get to travel to exotic places, the names of which I can't even spell, work from anywhere in the world, and get paid to be my own lady-boss. I have completely transformed my life and am now the founder of an incredible company designed to support women on their journey to self-empowerment.

I am on a mission to empower spirited women to turn their wounds into their greatest strength by unleashing their full potential hidden under layers of 'not good enough,' so they can pursue what sets their soul on fire. I give them wings and watch them soar as they claim their goddess status, manifest money out of thin air, attract their soul-mates, fulfil their soul's purpose, conquer the world, and make their childhood dreams a reality. I radically transform their lives inside-out by bringing them back to themselves and grounding them in what is true for them.

For the first time in my life, I feel like I can be who I choose to be in any given moment. I get to be me, and most importantly, I get paid to be ME! I have finally awakened to my true identity and wake up every day celebrating ALL of me, celebrating all of life in its shining glory!

Deep down, I always knew I was 'enough.' I just forgot. I forgot that I was powerful beyond measure.

All this suffering has a purpose. Sometimes our lives are illuminated by clarity so bright, that we have no choice but walk into the light! I had no choice but to turn all this suffering into what is now my superpower - an inner power and confidence that are not dependent on people, circumstances, or events, because my inner awareness has arrived.

Being yourself in the world that desperately wants you to become someone you are not is not easy, but it's the only way to live life!

Sandra Stachowicz is a Transformational and Empowerment Coach for women, a Visionary, a Change-Maker, and the founder of *Awaken Inner Goddess*. She is on a mission to empower women to claim back their power, own their greatness, and reconnect with who they REALLY are at their core, not the story they made up! She believes in transforming the world one spirited woman at a time, by empowering women to live on their terms by unleashing their full potential, hidden under layers of fear, doubt, and insecurities.

She is a free spirit, intuitive, psychic, introverted, and a gypsy at heart. Most of all, she believes in awakening to your true identity by unlearning and unbecoming everything that you AREN'T, simply because being yourself is ALWAYS more than enough.

She built three businesses by the age of 30, and was a featured speaker in *The Business Woman's Guide to Success*. Her story was featured in the book, *Freedom Chicks,* about how inspiring women escaped the 9 to 5 grind and became successful entrepreneurs. If you want to learn more about Sandra or desire to work with her, visit www.awakeninnergoddess.com or email sandra@awakeninnergoddess.com.

Time Brings a Change

By Zinna Ary-Davis

While on my journey to discovering my authentic self, I came to realize, "Who I Am." I am a loving, caring, family-oriented, country-living woman, and I do not allow my past to control my destiny.

You may ask yourself, who am I to give advice, motivate, and to tell anyone that time brings change? I was the woman who wore a mask, not wanting the world to see the pain and hurt that transpired throughout my past that led to fear, insecurities, and doubt. A rape victim, drop-out, and non-achiever, I still held my head high because I knew my journey was just beginning. Now I am willing to share how time and forgiving myself and others changed my life for the good. Prayer and repentance led me to clean out my Pandora's Box of negative people and situations that happened in my past. Time allowed me to cut the umbilical cord that tied me to the men who raped me from the time I was a young girl to my adulthood. Until that moment, I had blamed myself, thinking there was something I needed to change about myself. But once I cut the umbilical cord, I was able to forgive these men that caused the hurt that led me on the path to low self-esteem, broken trust, abandonment and social issues, resentment, loss of dignity, self-disrespect, and break-ups. But most of all, I was able to forgive myself.

Even though I have had many negative impacts, people, and situations in my life, I didn't give up. I had to understand that the negative encounters were preparing me for my grand shift. Because once I forgave the people and myself, my shame was transformed into the courage to help other who had similar situations. I continued to have urges as if my old dreams and goals were being re-birthed inside of me.

These birth pains, however, created another shift in my life that led me to go back to school and earn my GED, and to go to college and obtain my degrees in Behavioral Science and Science Communication. I wanted to learn about my own behavior patterns because I thought I had to change something about myself. I wanted to write a book to help others achieve positive outcomes and overcome the things in their lives that have paralyzed them from achieving their dreams. Cleaning out my Pandora's Box of negative people and situations, as well as forgiveness created a positive shift that helped me realize that time brings a change.

Now, I would like to share with you how I cleaned out my Pandora's Box of negative people and situations. Your Pandora's Box is located deep inside you. And like the Pandora's Box of Greek myths, it is filled with many evils. It is the area where your hurt, pain, shame, and guilt are usually stored in the center of your stomach.

A toxic person or situation can come into your life through unforgiveness, resentment, hatred, and by allowing that person to label you. Remember, this is the first reason why forgiveness of others and yourself is extremely important. I understand that it is hard to forgive some people or situations. But, you must stay focused on your goal to remove all the people and situations that have come into your life and paralyzed you in certain areas. Yet, the harder it is to forgive, the bigger the dream or goal that you can achieve will be. I use my horrific experiences to help others. I show them how to overcome their setbacks and understand how we attract these harmful situations and people in our lives.

When I was a young girl, I was molested by an old man. Like so many, I was told, if you say something you will get in trouble not once, but twice, first by your parents and then by him. I was scared, and I never said anything. He rewarded me with candy, ice cream, and money, but I felt dirty and nasty. Still, I never said a word because he convinced me that no one would believe me. I became angry inside as a little girl, and cried every time this took place. I kept it a secret and stored it in my Pandora's Box. When I got older, another man did the same thing to me, and I became angry at him. I cried out to God and asked Him why would He allow this to happen to me?

Several years later, another man raped me, and I hated him. Yet, this was the very first time I remember asking God to forgive me for whatever I had done to cause this to happen to me. Two days later, this man was killed by someone else. I realized then the power of forgiveness, for myself and others. When I started forgiving people from my childhood, I started to get my power back and my voice became stronger and firm. When I see some of these men now, I can hold my head up. Therefore, I would like to share that the power of forgiveness over time will bring a change for your good. If you make a choice not to forgive then you will continue to attract the same types of people and situations.

Before my transformation could manifest, I had to call all the people that hurt me and tell them I was sorry. This call was confusing to many of them; they did not understand where this apology was coming from. I knew I never did anything to cause these men to molest me, and I never received a single apology from anyone. But, I also knew that by asking for forgiveness and forgiving them, I would be free. These phone calls were the beginning of my healing process, freeing me from the old, releasing it all, and regaining my powers, I was ready to start on my new journey.

I know forgiving someone who wronged you seems hard. When I apologized I started crying and had to crawl outside for some fresh air, because I could not breathe from crying so hard. I knew the molestation was not my fault, nor did I do anything to deserve it. But, when I stopped crying, it was as if a huge mountain was lifted from me. I no longer felt numb on the inside; when I laughed it was genuine. At that very moment my senses were awakened. I felt like a new person. I know if you genuinely forgive anyone, without expecting an apology, you will free yourself. Your dreams and aspiration will be awakened again. Time will bring a change for your good.

You do not have to look in your Pandora's Box if you want to remain in the same place where you are. But if you want to step beyond where you are, then you really must look inside yourself and do a true self-evaluation, forgiving people and situations that had a negative impact on your life. You must self-correct all the areas where there was hurt, pain, and self-blame. You are the only one who can do this self-correction. The real correction is to arrive at a new conclusion about wrong decisions you may have made in the past.

Does this seem overwhelming? Here is some good news: You only must correct one thing at a time, and I promise you will start seeing and experiencing a change in your life as time moves forward and you continue to clean out your Pandora's Box of negative situations, people, and self-blame. The hardest part of this process may be to forgive yourself when you know that you have not done anything wrong. For me, the hardest part was asking someone that hurt me to forgive me and not get an apology back. But, I had to ask for forgiveness because I had evil thoughts for this person and hate in my heart for all the people that hurt me. I had to be true to myself and take full responsibility of my thoughts as well. You must choose to become responsible for your own Pandora's Box.

You would be well advised to take out of your Pandora's Box the idea of blaming anyone else for your choices, or the problems you have in your life. If you really want to manifest time bringing a change in your life, make this decision and say, "I will never blame another person for anything. This is the last day in my life that I will ever blame anyone else for what I must handle in my life. I will assume and accept full responsibility for it – whatever it may be – without resentment or reserve towards anyone or myself. And if I cannot quite see how I made it happen, I know that being individually responsible, I can fix it."

You may have held on to other people's negative baggage in your being, and therefore you attracted the same things and situations in your life. What happened to you or what someone did to you is not your fault, but it is your responsibility to remove the blame from your Pandora's Box. This cleansing allows you to become a creator; you will no longer be the victim of the opposing behavior of others. Nor will you carry the negative situations that attract more critical experiences or negative people.

I was a drop-out from high school. Yet, after cleaning out my Pandora's Box of damaging experiences and cutting the umbilical cord of negative people and situations that hindered me, I realized I had to make amends with my past life. I went back to school and obtained my GED, then went straight to college at the age of thirty-seven. I just graduated this past May with a degree in Behavioral Science/Science Communication. Having my degree inspired me to pursue my dream of giving service to others by helping them reach their top potential, and being open about my own past, in hope that it would give confidence to others. When I walked across that graduation stage, I knew I was not that young girl that dropped out of school. I felt a sense of accomplishment instead of shame about part of my life that I didn't want anyone to know about.

Whenever I have a task that seems too big, I learned if I do not give up, I will be able to achieve anything I ever dream. My transformation is how I know that time brings a change.

While I was on my journey of going back to school, I realized I had a book inside me that wanted to come out. I started working on the book in 2007, but, I knew this endeavor would require me to hire a ghostwriter. Because I was in college with twelve to fifteen credit hours a semester, I was not going to have enough time. I really didn't know where to start, but I continued to feel strong urgings to write this book, and I wanted it out. I paid a ghostwriter and hired an editor who found a lot of errors my ghostwriter made. When I went back to her, she told me that she would fix the errors for two-hundred dollars more. I felt like that price was unfair in my heart, since she made the errors. I became more discouraged and wanted to give up. Instead I refused to give the ghostwriter any more money. I sent the book back to the editor, who finished editing the book and returned the final copy to me. But, at the end of the editing she wrote, "P.S. This is not a good book." These six words became my setback for about a year. I knew I had a book inside me, but even those closest to me said I couldn't do it, and that I would never be good at anything. To have a total stranger affirm this negative idea was very hurtful.

Then, I prayed and found a Business coach on Facebook. She was an inspiration, and I sent her a copy of my book. She gave me a call, and as we talked, I thought I was ready to move forward. At first, I did not stay committed, because I recognized that I had not forgiven the other people who took advantage of me, nor did I forgive the editor who said harsh words to me. So, again I had to de-clutter my Pandora's Box of these negative situations. I had to say each person's name out loud as I forgave them for how they made me feel, how they tried to take advantage of me, and their harsh words. Once you start the process of forgiveness, every negative person and situation from your past comes up in your head. Forgive them again because you remembered them for a reason. Revisiting the past is not always easy, but it will be rewarding for you. Forgiveness allowed me to reconnect to the Business coach, and I have stayed committed to co-authoring this book.

Therefore, my message to you is that Time Brings a Change. I know where I've been, what I have accomplished, and who I've become. My past doesn't have control over me; I have control over my past. Don't allow other people to label you by your past. Judgment will not stop, so keep pressing forward. Always remember you have the last say-so in the outcome of your destiny. Keep in your heart that you can't always depend on people to be loyal, so have faith in yourself and believe in you. Be authentic, giving yourself permission to trust in yourself, believe in yourself, and love yourself. With hard work, self-elevation, and dedication I know, that Time Brings a Change.

Zinna Ary-Davis was born in Louisiana. Zinna really enjoys motivating others, and she has a gift to awaken the dormant personality inside of people who do not believe in themselves or have endured situation that have taken their toll. She believes in helping others, because throughout the years she learned how to deal with individuals accordingly. When she was going through her own setbacks, she did not give up. Instead, she started helping other people to be successful in achieving their dreams. Just being of service to others is how she gets her joy. She knows that there is enough success and prosperity in the universe for all of us to achieve our dreams and take our place in having a positive impact on the world. She is a person that made a commitment to help others achieve their goals for the long haul.

She is a loving, caring, family-oriented, country-living woman.

If you think you need more help on your journey than you can provide on your own, please visit Zinna's personal Facebook page or her website. You can send her a private message, and she will respond to your message in a timely manner to help you, because she cares.

https://www.facebook.com/zinna.davis?fref=ts

www.motivationalcoachz.com

Creating and Rising Above the Chaos

By Curtis G. Marsh

By definition, and possibly by your own experience, the word chaos signifies the greatest destruction and havoc, destroying so much in its path, that it should be avoided at all cost. Chaos seems to cause irreversible damage, and is a force that can consume and destroy even the greatest people, places, relationships, and businesses in the world.

So, let's define CHAOS.

One of the many definitions of chaos is: *complete confusion and disorder: a state in which behavior and events are not controlled by anything* (Merriam Webster)

So, what does chaos have to do with being or becoming a significant entrepreneur in a world of so much sameness and order? In my opinion, it is one of the most critical factors for your own personal and business success. Please take note; I said personal AND business success. The two are very much connected, and the choices, reactions, and core values you have in your personal life will become coupled with your business life. I also guarantee that your business and personal life have the potential to personally destroy you.

Let me take you back to my very humble beginnings…

I was blessed to be born into a middle-class family as the first-born son, to what would later become a family of four children. I still have those two amazing parents in my life today, and am grateful for all that they have taught me through experience and tough love. We lived on the 'tough side' of town, and my father worked several jobs while going to the University of Utah where he later received his Master's degree in Elementary Education. My mother supported my father by raising us four children, all of whom were just 18 months apart.

We had tremendous balance in our family, balance in all things that made up the Norman Rockwell vision of a perfect American family.

My first and earliest lessons about entrepreneurship were learned as I watched my dad dedicate and commit to not only his schooling and career, but to his family, community, faith, and spiritual beliefs.

I learned through personal experience as I worked with many charities, that we are actually the receiver when we give to others.

All of these pieces, a strong commitment to family, community, and giving back, as well as solid faith and spiritual beliefs, are critical to success in both personal and business areas.

My dad had a 'WHY,' that was unwavering: his family, legacy, and desire to serve and give back to others. He measured his life and means by taking a stand for something and then living his life in alignment with it. Ultimately, living with purpose means focusing on things that matter. If you do not have a 'WHY,' I don't care HOW and WHAT you do, your success will fall short and have very little significant impact and meaning.

You must first start with your passionate 'WHY.' There are no shortcuts to success.

I worked side-by-side with my dad for many years to learn all that I could. He was a great mentor, teacher, and loving father. I learned many life lessons from my dad, but as the first-born, and a bit of a rebel, I was always looking to do things differently. So, I adopted the mindset of, 'Dare to Be Different.'

"There has got to be a better way," I always thought. "If only it was done this way (my way), the results would be so much more impactful and significant."

I wanted to break and redesign the rules of business and success, but many of those principals could not be broken because they have been proven to work, time and time again. There are laws in life that are both temporal and spiritual and carry with them irrevocable blessings or consequences.

Some rules are meant to be broken, some are not.

There comes a time in all of our lives when we want to break out of the status quo and raise the bar of success all on our own. This strong urge happened to me at the age of 20. I moved out of that humble and grateful mindset I was taught, and soon replaced it with a cocky and arrogant disposition which quickly took my life out of alignment with my core values. All of these choices would later prove to be chaotic and destructive in my life. However, like a slow leak, we seldom see the demise coming. The choices that we make accumulate, and I collected choices with irrevocable consequences that would later catch up with me.

What choices are you currently making in your personal and business life? Do they come with irrevocable blessings or consequences? Check yourself. Check your personal inventory and your 'WHY.' Check all of it often.

At the age of 20, along with my father, I built and grew a training program that taught others how to pass their test for Life, Health, and Securities licenses. I developed curriculum and hired instructors, marketed, and opened training facilities from Logan, Utah to Las Vegas, Nevada.

Under my leadership, enrollment expanded from eight students a month, to well over 200 students and six teaching locations. This 20-year old quickly got caught up in the worldly definition of success. After all, I believed that it was money and possessions that mattered most, and that was how the world measured success.

Yet, I lost what truly mattered most, and the humility, giving attitude, gratitude, belief, and trust in God slowly gave way to an arrogant monster.

I took credit for all of my success. What a lie I started to live. I created some positive chaos to make change happen in the starving business I acquired. Chaos is good in many ways. We need to create chaos to generate new beginnings. Change. Disrupt. Disturb a business that is flat-lining, so we can add life and give birth to a new dancing star.

I felt the balance in my life flitting away, but I was making money, so who really cared? I didn't. The world defined what they felt success was, and I perfectly fit the mold. I liked it, but success became the god I worshipped.

Greed became good, and I continued to feed it by wanting more and more of that worldly success. What I didn't know then, that I know now is that everything is temporary.

In my third year with this venture, I went to my dad who had trained me and asked for more shares and ownership. We discussed the significant growth I had produced, and plans for the future.

After hours of a head-to-head battle with my dad, as he listened and counter-attacked, I told him just how great I was. I never once gave him credit for starting the business. I took all the acclaim at how successful I made this venture.

He thanked me for my efforts, but after hearing enough of my arrogance and attitude, he leaned over his desk and softly said to me, "With that attitude, you will never amount to anything. Furthermore, you also will never amount to anything without me."

I smirked and looked him straight in the eye, saying, "Watch me!!"

His reply, as a father teaching a life lesson, was, "Good Luck!!"

That statement was the stimulus I needed, and I decided to create some more chaos. It was a kick in the butt…it pissed me off, and I stormed out the front doors of his building.

"I'll show him," I mumbled under my breath.

I should have been humbled, but I was fired up and determined to prove my dad wrong. After all, what the hell did he know?

At 23-years old, I went and demanded to see the Managing Director of the largest firm on Wall Street…Shearson-Lehman Brothers. I went to the big boys first because I had something to prove. I was in my first year at the University of Utah, studying for my Business Degree, but I felt school was a waste of time.

I got the meeting with the Managing Director, but he said that they wouldn't hire anyone under 27 or without a college degree. The words of my dad were still fresh in my head, and I was not going to leave there without an opportunity to prove myself. That rebel attitude still burned inside me.

Out of the 277 applicants for the title of Financial Consultant…I got the position.

I became the youngest Financial Consultant ever hired by Shearson-Lehman Brothers. It was again time, as a rebel entrepreneur, to create constructive and significant chaos.

I was newly married, no kids, and now on a purely commission-paying job. My new bride was not happy to say the least. She wanted that 'comfort zone' that is truly 'uncomfortable' for a rebel entrepreneur like me. I made $80,000 my first year, and the ego and arrogance accelerated, full-throttle.

I was the man…or at least so I thought. But, all things are temporary, and the values you possess, as well as your 'WHY," need to be in complete alignment for true success. Mine begin to separate. But did it really matter? I was living the ultimate dream with all the world's definition of success that came with it.

From the age of 23 to 43, I experienced more success, dined with more celebrities, played all the most coveted golf courses, traveled to places I would have never dreamed of, made more money, and played harder than I could have imagined. This time in my journey was truly a story that I was writing, and there wasn't anything I couldn't accomplish.

It was the ride of my life.

There are so many things I was proud of, and many I was not so proud of...but they all have shaped me. I will say that chaos was created during this time of my life. Some was used to cause creative change, while other chaos left me in the wake of its destruction. It was all a choice on my part.

Fast forward to January 8th 2008.

I had been blessed to financially retire from my Wall Street and Investment career two years previously. I had it all, as defined by the world, and it was time to try and keep my beautiful family together. I was now on my second marriage, since I blew up my first one due to choices, misalignment, pride, and arrogance. I had two adorable daughters that were the greatest blessing in my life. I had become a liar to cover up my lifestyle that did not align with my core values and beliefs. I lost my inner peace which is what generates true wealth. On the outside I appeared to be a wealthy and blessed man, but on the inside, I was in total destructive chaos. I had fed the wrong values, and now I was suffering for that. Money and material possessions could not buy what I so badly needed...inner peace.

On the morning of January 8, I stepped into divorce court for the second time at the age of 43. I was about to begin two days of an ugly divorce battle that I was certain I would win. After all, I had the power, attorneys, and money. I was not going to lose. I came to win and brought all that arrogance, ego, and anger into the courtroom.

After the conclusion of the second day of intense fighting between her attorney and me, I'd had enough of the rules and the system. I had battled in many Wall Street and business negotiations, and won, so I believed that releasing the most powerful and intensely disrespectful tirade ever seen in that courtroom would help me win my case. But I was sorely mistaken.

How do I know? The judge told me so as he slammed down his hand on his bench and shouted, "That is the most egregious thing I have ever had said in my courtroom, and you are the most egregious man I have met in 18 years on the bench!"

He wasn't finished teaching me what I now consider one of the greatest lessons of my life so far.

"You just got yourself 30 days in jail for contempt!" he shouted.

"Good, I have money, I will bail!!" I shouted back as three large Bailiffs begin the process of handcuffing me and preparing me for my incarceration.

"No Bail!" he screamed.

"Don't worry about it, I know people!!" I screamed back.

I spent the full 30 days in jail.

These were the worst, yet the best 30 days of my life, because I truly needed to slow down and find my 'WHY,' core values, and beliefs. Trust me, I don't recommend this method. It is for this reason I share my story, in order to help you rise above the chaos that we create if we do not stay aligned with our personal core values and beliefs. Your personal life will be destroyed, as well as your business success if you fail to keep in alignment and don't give gratitude to what got you there, or to the God who blessed you with each and every single one of your talents.

As an entrepreneur our success is based upon many things.

There are those academic lessons that we learn from Universities and books, and others that come from practical application and experience. We must generate constructive chaos, and find ways to rise above our broken ways of doing things in business. Create that necessary change in order to produce a new beginning.

There is Order in the Chaos if we seek it.

As entrepreneurs, we also create our own destructive chaos which can shake even the strongest foundation of personal and family life. Order is all about core values and seeking balance. Stay in alignment, be generous with others, because it is a natural law in life the giver is also the receiver, and I guarantee you will have the greatest success both personally and in business as an entrepreneur.

Align with your WHY and your core values both personally and professionally on a daily basis. It is all about our choices, owning them, and rising above the chaos in our lives. As an entrepreneur you have to both create and rise above the chaos.

I have pressure-tested life and it works. I live it full-throttle.

Love, Honor, and Respect is my creed.

I wish you enough.

Born and raised in Bountiful, Utah, Curtis G. Marsh quickly realized the miracle and power behind "Paying it Forward." The avenues of success were opened to Marsh as he sought first to help others. In 1985, Marsh became the youngest Financial Advisor ever hired by Wall Street's top leading firms, Shearson-Lehman Brothers. Blessed with the skill sets he credits his Mother and Father for, he saw no limits to what he felt he could accomplish.

During the Stock Market crash of 1987, he learned one of life's greatest lessons…monetary wealth was not the true way to add value to one's life. His shift towards giving time and energy to charities was how he determined he would add value to others. Marsh, along with his clients, began a journey that lifted others, and pushed him to personal and professional success.

He is now one of the largest individual fund raisers in the country. The Muscular Dystrophy Association, Anasazi Foundation, and Make-A-Wish Foundation became his focus and passion.

Marsh resigned as a Senior Vice President from Janus Capital Group in 2006, and started Capital Growth Management, Inc., which he currently runs as President and C.E.O. Charities/Foundations and fundraising are divisions of his pursuits. Currently residing in Farmington, Utah, Curtis spends his time with his two daughters, enjoying the outdoors, and pursuing his passion for riding Harley Davidson motorcycles.

You may find out more about Curtis or contact him at www.CGMWealthAdvisors.com

Now that you've read these amazing stories, how would you like to be part of the next anthology project and spread your message worldwide?

All you have to do is turn in your story and I'm going to give you easy-to-follow steps to writing it so that it speaks to those people who need your help. I'm also going to take away the tech overwhelm by publishing the book for you and guaranteeing the Best Seller status. Plus, I'm even going to have your story edited by my team.

➔ **Go here for details on the next project** – join or get on the waiting list: http://bit.ly/nextanthology

* * * * * * * * * * * * * * *

What's it like being in an anthology like this one?
Just see what the co-authors of this book say …..

Being a part of this Anthology has been one the most rewarding experiences I have had as an author. I really appreciate the organization, the positivity and the encouragement that was shared. Vickie – it has been an absolute pleasure working with you! I learned so much! I cannot wait to meet you face to face so we can go shoe shopping! Keep doing what you do! You are truly a blessing.

~ Dr. Joy Lough, Founder/ CEO of Joy Lough Enterprises, LLC, Journey Coach

* * * * * * *

I have always loved to create and share stories, especially those with a Little Lesson of Life that can inspire others in their journey. I have never thought of myself as a writer, and publishing a book was not something I would have ever pursed on my own. Vickie Gould changed this for me and opened the path for me to share my hidden treasures with the world.

I have now published two books with Vickie's assistance and it has been a simple and rewarding journey each time. Now is your time. Write your stories and Vickie will walk the journey of publishing with you. I plan to share so much more with the world and I know I can because of Vickie.

~ Brooks Gibbs, Author & Mentor

* * * * * * *

A dream to me published can true when I joined the Anthology. You can say that I "rose above" a belief that it should be difficult and complicated. It was instead an easy, supportive and inspiring experience.

~ Laverne Wyatt,

* * * * * * *

➔ **Go here for details on the next project** – join or get on the waiting list: http://bit.ly/nextanthology

I can't wait to meet you!

Vickie Gould

www.ingramcontent.com/pod-product-compliance
Lightning Source LLC
Chambersburg PA
CBHW070143230526
45471CB00002B/500